FLOURISH

To my amazing friends and family, without your support and daily encouragement I would never have been able to write this book x

FLOURISH

MEGAN WELLMAN

First published in Great Britain in 2023 by Amazon.

Copyright © Megan Wellman 2023

The right of Megan Wellman to be identified as the Author of the Work has been asserted by her in accordance with the Copyright, Designs and Patents Act 1998.

All rights reserved. No part of this publication may be reproduced, stored in a retrieval system, or transmitted, in any form or by any means without the prior written permission of the publisher, nor be otherwise circulated in any form of binding or cover other than that in which is it published and without a similar condition being imposed on the subsequent purchaser.

ISBN: 9798863257679
Imprint: Independently published

www.meganwellman.com

FLOURISH

Table of Contents
Introduction
Understanding White Privilege
The Ingrained System
Black Children of White Countries
Africa and Europe: A little bit of history
Entering the Working World
Western European Beauty Standards
Professional Hairstyles
Looking the Part
Going the Extra Mile
Writing Your CV
Cover Letter Tips
Interview Tips
The Follow-Up
Handling Rejections
Difficult Conversations You May Have
Staying True to Yourself (Be Your Authentic Self)
Finance Template
Benefits of Gratitude, Planning and Journaling
Glossary of Terms
101 Black Owned Businesses you can shop from
References

To the reader,

In 2020, after the increase in support for the #BlackLivesMatter movement, I thought long and hard about how I felt the colour of my skin impacted me most. I came to the conclusion that it had been during my time in schools and workplaces.

The average person spends 90,000 hours in their workplace in their lifetime.

So I started writing. I started writing about what I saw in advertising campaigns and about how we can all make everyone feel more comfortable in the workplace. I believe everybody should have access to opportunities that allow them to elevate themselves, and their career, no matter their heritage.

I hope as you navigate your way through this book it helps to put yourself in the best position possible as you transition through life, from school or college and into the workplace embarking on new adventures that are positively conducive to your life experience.

In this book, I have tried to contain all of the information that I wish I was told as a fourteen year old girl when I was told to choose the GCSE's I needed that would determine my future, and then as I entered the working world.

This comprehensive handbook should guide you on your journey as you navigate new situations and will help you understand what the early stages of your career is going to be like.

You'll find a *Notes* section towards the end so if you're inspired with any ideas whilst reading, you can write them down right away.

This process has been a challenging one for me personally, which has taken significant introspection, that meant reliving some distressing experiences that may be triggering for you.

But most of all, I hope you find this as useful in your life as I have found writing it, and that you learn and gain the confidence to Flourish.

Megan x

Understanding White Privilege

Before you even start thinking about your career prospects and what you want to do once you finish education, it's imperative to understand what white privilege is (and how that can impact you) as a person who doesn't have white skin living in a country where the vast majority of people do.

According to Oxford Languages, the term white privilege is the "inherent advantage possessed by a White person on the basis of their race in a society characterised by racial inequality and injustice."
Effectively, this means that if you are White (part of the majority ethnicity) then your skin colour will most likely not be used against you. Your skin colour is unlikely to make your life any harder. Your skin colour is considered the norm and anything that deviates from that is 'different'.

This isn't a generalisation that the majority race in Western countries has an easy life and hasn't experienced distressing experiences related to being different, it just means that your skin colour in particular doesn't inherently agitate experiences that they normally wouldn't.

2020 will go down in history as the year that marked the start of a global pandemic that most people thought could only happen in fictional dystopian movies. The

Western world, however, was already trapped in what British journalist Reni Eddo-Lodge, in the closing pages of her book 'Why I'm No Longer Talking to White People about Race', defined as a real "horror movie".

Before that; Brexit, the election of Trump, the growth of xenophobic and fascist parties across Europe, and the proliferation of conspiracy theories on "ethnic substitution" and "white genocide" are just some of the more disturbing scenes that were once seen as extremism. Temporarily, in the shade of the first months of the pandemic, racial aggravation in the United States returned to the forefront following George Floyd's murder in police custody and the assault on the Capitol on January 6, 2021, characterised by the uniform Whiteness of the perpetrators.

Videos were circulating social media of guards openly allowing protestors to enter the Capitol building. Knowing the extent of police brutality, how many citizen fatalities there would have been, had the participants of the Capitol storming been Black?

There are countless videos of Black people being treated unfairly by other citizens, police and people in positions of power across social media every day. It's hard to explain how it feels waking up to something new on social media almost every day, and one of the underlying reasons people act in horrific ways is because they believe you are less of a person because of the colour of your skin.

In the working environment, White Privilege can be masked as innocent favouritism of an employee, or certain work activities that only seem to be tailored to one culture. It can be hard to recognise it early on, but once you know what to look out for, it will be easier for you to choose the right workplace for you.

The Ingrained System

Unfortunately, it's human nature that when the majority race often talk about racism (if they even recognise its existence) it largely centres around sensational acts of violence or extremism and refers to outlandish statements such as "Black people don't want equality, they want to take over". There is something deeply wrong with this view because racism is not made up of isolated episodes. It's a system in which Black people are at an inherent disadvantage and from which White people (everyone, even if they are not racist) naturally benefit from.

In life, you will come across people who deny racism, and say things such as "I don't see colour, I treat everyone equally". For a start, we don't want equality right now, we need equity. But also, it's not enough to say "I'm not racist", you need to be actively anti-racist, and courageously call out those behaviours in others and unjust systems so we can all live in a fair and harmonious society.

What we need to understand (and by we, I mean everybody) is the systemic racism that has existed, and continues to exist in our world - which many people fail to see just because they haven't experienced it. My first experience of racism (that I remember at least) was when I was 12 years old. A friend of mine (who was White) was upset that I had made a new group of friends and called me a N****r. Hard R. Multiple times. I was devastated, and so my mum called the Police. I printed out the conversations between us and handed them over, the Police took them to her house and came back and said they won't be pursuing things further because they believe her mum will punish her?

That experience showed me early on how people can say what they want, regardless of the harm done, without serious consequence. Following this was a string of experiences over many years that made me completely lose faith in the institutions that we operate in day-to-day, from the workplaces, to the housing market, to banking and insurance too.

It is time for parents to teach young people early on that in diversity, there is beauty, and there is strength.

~ Maya Angelou

Black Children of White Countries

I'm mixed White British and for most of my life thought British Caribbean (Dominica). There isn't much in the way of historical documentation for the Black side of my family. I've spent many hours researching and investigating to find out my ancestors are from Nigeria, and were then sold as slaves to work on British Sugar Plantations across the Caribbean, where my grandparents were born. They came to the UK during Windrush, had their children, and then later settled in Dominica.

I am constantly asked where I'm from, "where I'm really from", and yeah but where was I born. I can confirm, all England. I was born here, and I was raised here. Questions about my heritage and ancestry would have a different answer. I've also been questioned on whether I was telling the truth, and that I speak very good English?!

I've grown up in a White country that rejects Blackness. I am considered light-skinned. I've previously been rejected by Black communities and been called a "Coconut" or that I'm "really White", I've faced so many counts of racism from White communities, and growing up there were not many mixed Black people around me. Luckily, as I've gotten older I know myself more and have friends from lots of different backgrounds and I feel very welcome across many communities.

My age group is really the first generation of children born from interracial relationships. Everything has been new. I'm aware I benefit from Colourism, being western society's accepted version of a Black woman (even though I am not 100% Black), but still get the racism, and struggle to know my place. All I know right now, is that if I am the accepted voice, I will do everything I can to amplify others.

Another thing is that with 82% of the UK population being White, of course most of my friendships and romantic relationships are White people (not to mention half of my family). One thing I've had to battle with is people seem to perceive the way I talk and act as a "White person", when really - it's just British. I've had this battle with myself, do I act differently with Black friends? Am I different when I'm around the Black side of my family? The answer is yes. Here I am not talking about code-switching, I'm talking about being brought up in two cultures, and when I spend time with one, I lean into it more.

But relationships can be hard. I've had ex-boyfriends tell me they are not sure how their parents would react to them dating a mixed Black woman (that relationship swiftly ended) and men who have actually said the words "I'd love to get with a Black woman" EW. Not me. For so long, I felt when it came to 'my person' they should be Black. So many people had made me feel guilty for accepting the White side of myself, and this trickled its way down to my relationships. I felt I should make myself have more of a focus on Black men when I was dating, but life doesn't work that way. You fall in love with who you fall in love with. Your race and your skin colour should not dictate that. Your friendships and romantic relationships should be with people who accept you for who you are, and when you need them, will fight your corner too. Don't feel guilty for falling in love outside of your own race.

Unfortunately, there is a lot of stigma in some communities that you may come across on social media that talk about some races "stealing" partners from others. Interracial relationships are still new in some cultures, but it's important to not feel pressured because other people are not happy with their own situation. It can seem like the easy option to stay with someone within your own culture because they already understand your way of life, but how incredible is it to learn about and share new cultures. It can feel like having this internal battle with yourself every day when you are of mixed heritage growing up in a White country.

Africa and Europe: A brief history

The existence of Black European citizens is more recent than one might imagine. Proof of this is Olivette Otele, a historian of Cameroonian origin who grew up in France. By accurately telling the story of influential Black characters in Europe, but whose Blackness has been removed from the collective imagination or whose personality has been cloaked in an aura of extraordinariness, Otele questions the historical paradigm of exceptionalism. An approach that says a lot about the European outlook on Blackness: the positive evaluation attributed to some historical Black figures derives from the idea that they were exceptional characters, and that in some way their existence had been transformed precisely by the encounter with Europeans.

What is particularly original of European Africans is the choice of adopting a long-term vision. The history of relations between Africa and Europe does not begin, as often happens in many history manuals, with colonisation. Otele goes much further back, telling the stories of characters who can be considered to all intents and purposes Afro-Roman. An example above all is San Maurizio who, originally from the region between Egypt and Sudan, even became the patron saint of the Holy Roman Empire. Character representations of him suggest that his Blackness was not a problem for his contemporaries and for much of the Middle Ages. Subsequently, when the concept of race begins to take shape, the representations of the saint will suffer and the idea will spread that he was saved, despite being an African, because he was a Christian, thus becoming an exceptional individual. The historian then proposes a particularly interesting change of perspective, reflecting on the impact that Africa, the colonised continent, has had on Europe, the colonising continent. And this is where the stories of European Africans come into play:

"In addition to raw materials, artefacts and plants, the most visible and lasting mark that Africa has left on Europe is made up of people" - (Otele, 2021)

However, many of these people have never been fully considered part of the country in which they spent their existence, and have often been erased from national memories. In the eighteenth century in France, the returning colonisers, who returned with their children of double heritage, represented a problem, because they placed the cradle of the Enlightenment in front of its implication in the trafficking and exploitation of human beings, practices accepted in the colonies but which one preferred not to see in the motherland.

This is the case of Joseph Boulogne (1739, Guadeloupe-1799, Paris). The son of a French nobleman who owned plantations and an enslaved

Senegalese woman, he moved to France at the age of nine with his father and brother. Joseph's father believed that the best way to protect his son from his skin colour was to invest in an aristocratic upbringing. With the nickname "The Knight of Saint-Georges", Joseph became the most famous musician in France and with his concerts he attracted audiences from all European capitals. A few years after his death, Napoleon reestablished slavery in all the French colonies and banned the music of the knight of Saint-Georges; his story disappeared completely from national memory. It is only thanks to the French Afro-Caribbean communities that a street in Paris was named after him in 2001. And, finally, in 2014 in a public commemoration on the abolition of slavery.

Theodor Michael (1925-2019), on the other hand, was born in Germany to a colonial migrant of Cameroonian origin and a German woman, who died a year after his birth. Although he was German by birth, he was denied citizenship and in childhood he worked in human zoos that endorsed stereotypes about Africans. But his life "tells the success story of a man who managed to rise above class and race" (Otele, 2021). He was one of the few Afro-Europeans to have told it in autobiography, a text from which the identity struggle that characterises people of double heritage in Europe emerges:

"When people said 'we', they didn't mean me." And when I looked in the mirror I saw that it was just like that. […] I oscillated between rejection, doubt, hatred for myself and the pride of being different from others. […] I didn't have a single place in the world! Neither in German society, nor in Cameroon "

Theodor Michael thought that racism was a burden that racists had to bear, and in the last years of his life, thanks to the discovery of the Afro-German communities, made up mostly of younger generations, he was able to get out of the loneliness he had experienced, for much of its existence.

In the last parts of her volume Otele focuses precisely on the many Afro-European communities present in Europe today, and in particular on Black activism committed to documenting the Black presence in European history through collective production processes of knowledge.

"While in the eighteenth century almost all Afro-Europeans had to walk on tiptoe, reluctant to assert their presence, in the twenty-first century French Afro-feminists and other Afro-Europeans claim the right to define themselves, reshape the discourse about race, feminism and their same lives " (Otele, 2021).

It is mainly women who engage in these operations. Afrofeminists contest the idea that the (White) majority has the power to define the identities of minorities. Black scholars question universities' approaches to inclusion and diversity"and highlight the paradox of the absence of Black women in academic debates on equality.

Patriarchy and racism as political structures follow a similar logic, which is why many believe that White women are more likely to understand how racism works. However, in a seemingly contradictory way, it is precisely many White feminists who show themselves hostile in fighting the battle of racism. But this goes back to the whole "It's a man's world" concept, that the White man is the most powerful. White thinking has also been suggested to be masculine, as White women and women in general, have not had as much power as the White man has.

Reni Eddo-Lodge dedicates ample space to the relationship between feminism and whiteness. Feminism, she claims, is at the root of anti-racist thinking about her, because it has given her a mental framework to understand the world. Probably growing up in a society that makes Whiteness the norm, and that avoids naming the race as much as possible, makes it more immediate and less problematic to identify as a woman than as a Black person.

However, the author notes, while White people may defend their spaces and their one-colour world, some feminists have settled into Whiteness like anyone else. Feminism, they say, is not the place to discuss the racial question; as if the fact of being a woman could be separated from the fact of being Black. A clarification must be made: Eddo-Lodge does not believe that this attitude concerns all White feminists, but only those who manage to combine feminist politics with that of

Whiteness, which is a structurally racist politics. An oxymoronic union in her eyes:

"Feminism needs to demand a world that admits the existence of a racist history by taking responsibility for it, in which reparations are distributed equally, in which the concept of race is deconstructed from top to bottom. I am well aware that these demands are utopian and unrealistic. But I believe that feminism must be utopian and unrealistic, very far from the world we live in "- (Eddo-Lodge, 2021).

Taking the perspective of White privilege implies a reversal of the way we usually think of racism: seeing not only what happens to those who suffer it, but also and above all who benefits from it. What, then, is the responsibility of those who, while not engaging in racist practices and behaviours, find themselves in a privileged position, guaranteed by the very existence of racism? The primary responsibility is the reluctance, if not rejection, to listen to what Black people have to say about racism. Renni Eddo-Lodge's book "Why I'm No Longer Talking to White People About Race" is a title that could be deceiving, it seems to suggest that it is Reni Eddo-Lodge who wants to end the conversation about racism with White people. In reality, hers is a response to all those who do not intend to recognise the structural dimension of racism.

Facing White privilege is painful, and perhaps even embarrassing to some, because it "forces people who have never been responsible for active racism to deal with their complicity in its existence" (Eddo-Lodge, 2021). However, White people, especially those who intend to be anti-racist, perhaps have no other way at the moment than to accept the discomfort that comes with becoming aware, without pretending that there can be a quick and painless solution to racism; because this, the British journalist strongly states, is not possible at the moment.

Accepting discomfort does not in any way mean wallowing in feelings of guilt. After all, you can not help the position you were born into. I don't believe we should be pointing fingers and people, and "cancelling" them or sending hate to anybody. Education is key. We need to understand what racism actually is, so that ALL people can take charge of it. It's not just a matter of people accepting racism for what it is, it's accepting that White people have always, and continue to benefit from a racist system.

Any possible form of action must necessarily pass through this acceptance. To White people who have become aware of their privilege, and to whom this privilege "weighs like a stone", Eddo-Lodge suggests using it in many ways: providing administrative and economic support to anti-racist battles; talking about racism with other White people, using their voice in all places of power where it can be heard. All this can contribute so that no one is anymore "The Only Black Person in the Room" and to reopen the history of Europe to recognise within it a place that has been denied for too long, that of European Africans. Not all White people obviously wish to be anti-racist and the most cynical might wonder why, ultimately, White people should give up their privilege in favour of a fairer and more just world.

White thinking, the foundation of the resulting privilege, also has dire consequences for White people. It is a way of life that cannot survive without violence, without putting the most vulnerable on the margins of society. It is also functional to the exploitation of White people who are not in power: racism offers them an enemy so that they do not rebel against those who really exploit them.

Its consequences are much more extensive than one might imagine, as it does affect not only the power relations between people, but also the sustainability of human impact on Earth. White identity, like a Black identity, is also assigned. Learning to see it is an act of freedom.

Strength lies in differences, not in similarities.

~ Stephen Covey

Entering the Working World

As you leave school, college or university and embark on your chosen career path, you are likely to be joining a company and working for somebody else. You are also more likely to be managed by, or work at a company that is owned by a White person. It will be common for the leadership team to be made up by a majority of White people. You may not be in this situation, and have a diverse team around you, but there is a slim chance of this happening. Partly because of the demographic of the area you live in, partly due to structural racism. It's important for you to know that if you do end up in a company where this is the case, it doesn't mean you will have a hard time. Not all White people are racist, not all people are racist. But you may have to deal with cultural differences that you struggle with.

This is where you need to ensure you have the tools to succeed and exceed expectations in this environment. I want you to have the skills you need to help you navigate the workplace in a White world. The more work we put in now, means the less work the generation of Black and mixed Black people will need to do after us. It is unfair, that as ethnic minorities we have to go the extra mile and put in 10x the work to achieve the same recognition as a White person. But this is currently the world we live in. By going the extra mile now, and becoming CEOs, Managing Directors, Politicians, Popular Artists, we will be able to use our platforms, pave the way and make it easier for the next person trying to go on the same journey.

Why do Black people (and other minority ethnicities) need to work 10x harder to achieve the same recognition and opportunities you ask? This goes back through hundreds of years of oppression, slavery and racism that while illegal now, these beliefs have been passed through generations and generations of families.

According to Rich Lowry (editor of the National Review) Black Americans need to achieve three 'middle-class norms; coined the "success sequence" which are;
- Graduating from high (secondary) school
- Maintain full time employment or has a partner that does
- If you choose to have children, do so after marriage or after the age of 21

However even when following this list, ethnic minority economic prospects are still worse than those of White people.

Discrimination at work is not only unfair, but also harmful: if a company does not hire the best talent because of some prejudice about their appearance, sexual orientation, religion or gender, it benefits competitors. In practice, however, things go differently, and the studies we have available show that not only has it existed and still exists today almost everywhere, but also that it has a profound effect on the way in which individuals become part of companies.

There are so many statistics that show having diverse teams in the workplace actually benefits the company.

- Diversity and inclusion strategies reduces staff turnover risk by 50%
- Companies with diverse management teams have 19% higher revenue due to innovation
- Organisations with inclusive cultures are 1.7 times more likely to be innovation leaders in their market
- Inclusive teams make better business decisions up to 87% of the time

There have been numerous studies over the years that have shown companies discriminate against sexuality, race, religion, gender, age and more when it comes to candidate screening, interviews, job offers and promotions. Whilst there has been much more in the media that people are treated unfairly at work, it seems lots of people are talking about race, or having token diversity hires to appease, rather than to implement actual changes. We do see more companies sign up to programmes or working with consultancies in an effort to improve their diversity and their perhaps not so far procedures and processes - which is a positive. Explicit forms of racism are now significantly less common than they were in the past but still present in more subtle forms especially in the corporate setting. In the workplace, racial discrimination means unfavourable treatment of a candidate or employee, and other microaggressions.

A study that revealed the presence of discrimination at work evaluated employees in the United States, the United Kingdom, France and Germany that the phenomenon of racism is common in all states, albeit to varying degrees. Among the key findings of the survey: Adults employed in the United States are more likely to experience and witness discrimination (61%) than those in the United Kingdom (55%), France (43%) and Germany (37%). 42% of employed adults in the United States have experienced or witnessed racism in the workplace, the highest percentage of the four countries surveyed: the United Kingdom (37%), France (30%) and Germany (24%). Half (50%) of employed adults in the four countries believe their employer should do more to promote diversity and inclusion. The results of this survey should be a wake- up call for workers and employers to promote a more inclusive culture and thus put an end to any form of discrimination at work.

The paradox that emerges from the various research is that many companies claim diversity and inclusion are among their highest values, while perpetuating wage gaps, all-White leadership teams, and high turnover rates of Black employees . The American Psychological Association notes that the "victim effects" of racial discrimination include PTSD, depression and anxiety. Furthermore, a person's self-esteem and sense of self-efficacy are undermined, which from a working point of view translates into low performance, greater absenteeism and a high turnover rate.

At the time of writing this, I'm 26 and I have worked for 11 companies. I've been made redundant twice, and I have faced many racist encounters at work. Companies I have worked for that had affinity groups, which I was actually part of, did nothing when I complained about racist remarks made to me. Companies I've worked for, the CEO themselves have made racist and stereotypical jokes day in, day out. I would have to sit and listen as my White employees laughed at the jokes, whilst I sat there and found it anything but funny. I once called somebody out for saying something offensive about another employee, and I was questioned if I would have stuck up for my colleague if they didn't have brown skin.

There was an incident at work once where I went in with my hair in box braids, and somebody at the company told me I looked like Michonne from the Walking Dead. I didn't watch the programme, they asked me to pose with a figurine they had of her and post it to their social media. I felt uncomfortable when this happened but I wasn't really sure why - and I did not say anything.

They would not have known I was uncomfortable with this situation. It was only through education a few years later I understood this was a microaggression. I looked nothing like this woman, our facial features were not similar, she had Locs, I had Box Braids, she was dark skinned, I was light skinned. I then wrote about this experience on one of my Instagram accounts after I came to the conclusion it was a microaggression, and some people from the company (who did not follow the page) started bombarding my story poll of "Do I look like this person to you" with yes answers (even using their family's accounts). I explained all my thoughts in the caption, and instead of reading it and learning something, they removed all trace of me on their company social media, voted on my poll, and made no effort to reach out with a "Oh hey, let's talk about this!"

This caused me a tremendous amount of anxiety and I started questioning whether I should speak out about these situations. They clearly didn't read the full caption, I didn't name anybody. I later learned the person who started with the social media actually made a joke about Black people and fried chicken a few days later. They do say a leopard never changes its spots.

Both employers and employees have responsibility when it comes to promoting and monitoring diversity and inclusion policies in the workplace. Both stakeholders must work together to ensure the success of diversity initiatives in the company. Employers should act as facilitators and knowledge providers to improve employee relationships. They should also ensure the improvement of awareness of racial discrimination and ethnic diversity in the workplace.

Employees and organisations charged with protecting workers rights should lobby companies to ensure equal opportunities for all workers at all stages of the work cycle: from access to employment, to training, through career growth and retirement. Employees also play an important role in mutual awareness of the right to a workplace free from racial discrimination and in supporting their colleagues when concrete cases arise.

Ultimately, it is above all the responsibility of management to demonstrate its commitment to diversity and the value it brings to the company. Additionally, managers must actively communicate their position on racial discrimination and what will not be tolerated along with the consequences of the violation. Racism, in any form, should never be overlooked, excused or tolerated.

The first and most effective action an organisation can take to combat racism is to ensure that the most open, selfless and empathetic people (characteristics that generally make them less racist) end up being engaged in corporate diversity and inclusion. It is important that they take on leadership roles because they have the grit, the courage and the dedication to fight for a better status quo. In any organisation, change is more likely to happen from top to bottom, so leaders have the power to change people's beliefs and behaviours.

The second useful measure that companies should use to combat racism or any kind of discrimination is to "sanction" it. Corporate culture always includes both explicit and implicit rules for governing the interactions between its members, and it is the organisation's job to instil a culture of civility, respect and kindness. This is done through a long-term and systematic program aimed at creating an inclusive culture, in which minorities do not feel only "tolerated", but actually valued.

A culture where people are perceived as individuals rather than as group categories and where managers and employees are rewarded for strengthening this state through their daily actions.

What tools to put into practice?
1. Recruitment
Right from the first entry into the company and therefore in the choice of candidates, it is strategic to broaden the attention and interest in diversity of potential candidates.

2. Training
Training to promote anti-racism attitudes and behaviours is essential. But for it to be truly effective, employees must find the same attitudes, cultural messages and professed beliefs in the management system .

3. Company policy
It is vital to develop a written policy to help reduce racism in the workplace and enforce a strict tolerance for offenders. Corporate policies ensure that corporate values and philosophies can be balanced with good social responsibility.

4. Cultivate diversity and address unconscious bias
Many employers perpetuate racism in their workplace because they don't recognise the flaws in their internal corporate culture. Addressing unconscious prejudices with the help of a third party (often external to the company), and taking an honest look at one's own culture can help to minimise the constraints that prevent the culture from thriving.

Employers have the power to make a change and ensure that their workplaces operate on the basis of well-being and equality for all. They increasingly need to use that power to address the link between racism and mental health.

No human environment will ever be free from prejudice, but human organisations can do a lot to reduce discrimination in the workplace, including racism.

When you do find a job you love and you think you'd like to apply to, research research research. Check their website, check their social media platforms. Do they use a diverse range of people in pictures they use for advertising? Does their leadership team mirror this?

If you notice they use a lot of Black people in marketing, but this is not reflected in their team - why? You need to try and find out if this is a 'tick box exercise' for them, or if they really care about showcasing a range of people. Are they trying to show that they are dedicated to working on their diversity and inclusion?

Try to find out what the people who work for them are like. You can find the company on LinkedIn and use the 'people' tab to see who their current employees are. When you go to your interview, ask them how their workforce is made up.

If they have a great diverse range of employees, AMAZING. If not - ask them what their plans are in terms of recruitment. If they are uncomfortable discussing this, it is likely they are uncomfortable managing it, and therefore this is a 'red flag' that this could be a company you do not want to work for.

If they welcome this conversation and ask for your input, HURRAH. Whether you are offered the role or not, you have sparked the conversation. It's really important to do your research before you even apply for a job, as you don't want to end up working for a company that you're not happy with.

It's important to note that you may not be in the financial situation where you can choose which employer you work for.

You may need a job, and quickly. In this instance, sometimes you do need to take that stepping stone job.

If you do end up working for an employer that perhaps has had some 'red flags' when it comes to treating their employees in the right way and valuing them, you must ensure you have a good support network around you so if any issues arise, you know how to deal with them.

The Mini-Me Outbreak

As you start going in for interviews and meet employers, you may notice a lot of people having the same type of look. This is due to the 'mini-me' hire, that stops a lot of highly skilled minority ethnic people getting the roles they deserve.

Hiring managers are drawn to people that look like them, as opposed to the right person for the role. This will also happen when it comes to promotions. Managers tend to look for skills and personality traits they have themselves when it comes to promoting somebody, or someone who reminded them of them when they were trying to get their next promotion. This is not necessarily always on purpose, but it is very common.

It shouldn't be the case, but because of this it's very important to build relationships with your key stakeholders. These will be your colleagues who are at the same level as you, your line manager, their manager, your potential new manager and the CEO.

Colleagues at the same level;
If you go for a promotion, your manager will ask your colleagues for references. How well you work with them,

if they feel you will be right for the job, are you a good team player and more.

Your line manager;
This is the person who needs to recommend you for the promotion to your new potential manager. Make it clear that you can be managed well and don't need micro-management. That you exceed expectations and go above and beyond. If they will still be your manager after the promotion, show them you deserve it.

Your potential new manager;
Make yourself known to them. Establish a relationship and show an interest in their role and/or department. Show them that you care about what you do and have skills that would be right for them.

The CEO;
You never know how involved the CEO will be in projects or hiring. You must be able to hold a conversation and work with them. At the end of the day, any final decision will be theirs.

Building these relationships (and fulfilling the requirements of your job!) will ensure you are in the best position possible when it comes to going for a promotion.

Western European Beauty Standards

It may feel this isn't relevant to the working world - but it is. The typical look for a professional woman always goes to the mainstream, a White woman, and typically White features. Take note of the tweet that went viral a few years back, when googling unprofessional hairstyles, the images are all of Black women. When googling professional hairstyles, they are all of White women. It's understood that White women and White features and styles are the norms, and anything that deviates from that is different. The usual features are;

Having White skin
Being tall and skinny
Having straight long blonde hair
Having a small button upturned nose
Your breasts are on the larger side

Over recent years, Black culture has been more widely accepted and celebrated. Because of this, many White women (you'll see it in multiple celebrities including the likes of Kylie Jenner, Iggy Azalea, Jesy Nelson and more) have been getting enhancements on their bodies to get larger buttocks, thinner waists, and fuller lips - like a natural Black woman.

Whilst it's perfectly acceptable to make enhancements to your own body, many of these women have made themselves appear racially ambiguous. Which can be seen as offensive to ethnic minorities as they get the 'benefits' of the looks but still have White Privilege, and nothing that sets them back. They can also dissolve their fillers or remove their fake tan, essentially treating these features as disposable.

When you start working at a company, you may find yourself working with somebody who has done the very same thing. More and more people are appearing racially ambiguous and performing cultural appropriation rather than appreciation.

The vital thing is to stay true to yourself and your culture. If somebody is clearly blurring lines, it's okay to speak to them about it. Just treat them with the utmost respect and decency when having that conversation. There should be no accusations, just an open conversation. Some good ways to talk about this, if you're concerned somebody is making themselves appear racially ambiguous could be;

"Hey X, can we talk about something quite sensitive? I'd love to tell you a bit more about my heritage and where I come from, and learn more about yours"

This allows you to firstly understand if there is any part of their culture, that is part of the culture they **appear** to be appropriating. If it becomes clear that they are appropriating, you can continue with;

"That's really interesting that that's your background! I thought because of (appearance trait that is making them appear racially ambiguous e.g. a very serious and offensive dark tan coupled with wearing a coily wig) you had a mixed background. I think you are a beautiful person inside and out, and embracing who you are is so important. I know sometimes people can appear racially ambiguous when they aren't and it can cause some offence.

In my personal experience, it's not always a good idea as having only a few features of a minority ethnicity you don't get treated the same as someone who is an ethnic minority even though you benefit from their looks. I think as long as you appreciate the culture, but don't appropriate it, it's okay."

This will no doubt be an uncomfortable conversation, and you can word it in a way that suits you as a person. But it's up to you to have these conversations to create awareness for these situations, to try and reduce the amount that it happens.

Professional Hairstyles

Different hair types will require different hairstyles. In 2016 tweets went viral where people were searching the terms 'Unprofessional hairstyles' compared to 'Professional hairstyles' and were disgusted at the results. Only White people were coming up in the search under the professional term, and only Black people were coming up in the search under the unprofessional term. Illustrating just how ignorant and racist peoples opinions, (and apparently internet algorithms and SEO practices) can be. Coarse, curly, and Afro hair is NOT unprofessional! It is beautiful and there are so many ways to style it that will make you feel like a boss.

"Can I touch them?", "Have you ever straightened your hair?", "Do you have someone in your family with your hair?" are the most frequently asked questions that people with Afro textured hair hear very often. They may seem innocent questions, but in reality they hide behind a discriminatory world which carries with it many stigmatisation and stereotyped representations. And there is a term to describe this process: Hairism.

Midge Wilson, a professor of psychology and women's gender studies at DePaul University , said that in the

1960s, curly hair was conventionally accepted among whites, as was Afro hair for African Americans and Jewish people. The professor believes that they were synonymous with a wild and free spirit, but once the era of free love was over, this perception became a prejudice. She adds that, in pop culture, the most unbalanced women are represented with voluminous and dishevelled curls, while those serious and simple with well-groomed hair.

In an article for Cosmopolitan magazine, Anna Breslaw states that "In Hollywood, curly hair just isn't taken that seriously at work." As Saran Donahoo argues, Black women suffer a greater prejudice, because Afro hair is still a reason for discrimination and racist oppression that forces them to straighten their hair to follow the "White beauty norm". In the United States, in 2019, the Crown Act was passed, a law that, as Donahoo and Asia Danielle Smith affirm, seeks to support Black women and men in expressing their natural hair without fear of being discriminated against, fired, forced into greater "discipline" in schools, workplaces or public spaces.

Hairism is the term used to identify discrimination or prejudice based on hair, fueled by the "White beauty norm", that is, the preference for long straight hair to which most Black women, and not only, are subject. This type of discrimination classifies Afro hair as wrong, because it is unsightly compared to White/straight hair, the ideal of beauty. Furthermore, even among women who have decided to wear hairstyles to hide their natural hair, there is a social belief that they are more educated and sophisticated, therefore more competent in holding management positions.

The Crown Act, passed by eight states - California, Colorado, Connecticut, Maryland, New Jersey, New York, Virginia and Washington - identifies the fight against hairism as a matter of racial and civil rights. Policies and practices that label natural Black hairstyles as unprofessional and unwelcome violate The Civil Rights Acts of 1964.

In the UK, the 2010 Equality Act is supposed to prevent discrimination based on your race, which should extend to your hair if it's associated with your race or ethnicity. Even though the arguments supporting hair policies affect people of all ethnicities, Black women are the ones who suffer the worst effects of this discrimination. In the workplace they are 3.4 times more likely to have others perceive their natural hair as unprofessional, 1.5 times more likely to be fired for their hair, 80% more likely to decide to disguise their natural hair and twice as likely, compared to White women, to straighten their curls to fit the job.

However, these aspects affect the whole of society, not just the Black community. The principles of the Black feminist movement , the Combahee River Collective, argue that natural Black hair is above all a political issue because it affects the way a woman accesses and works in public spaces. For greater inclusion, it should be possible to extend the concept to the entire social fabric because not only in the Black community do we encounter prejudices that contain character stereotypes associated with the type of hair.

I myself can say that I come into contact almost every day with episodes of systemic racism, linked to my hair. This type of racism manifests itself, also through the use of negative or even derogatory terms in reference to curly hair. I realise this by reading certain newspaper articles, in the professional sphere and when I see how some hairdressers work. They, for example, are almost never interested in knowing and learning how to manage this category of hair; they refuse to offer a service to a large number of people (from whom they could make a nice profit!).

Unfortunately, I can say that afro hair experts can be counted on the fingers of one hand: in my local town there are very few hair stylists able to help curly girls to love their hair, able to give them a moment of pampering and relaxation. If you need to, search carefully: you will find people who, like me, want to offer you help. But wouldn't it be great if all these experts could find work in salons, collaborate and offer advice to those who ask for them? Yet in our country it does not happen.

I spent a few months in Tenerife as I work remotely. I booked an appointment in a salon to get my nails done, and whilst there I asked the hairdresser if they'd cut curly hair before and if I would be able to book in to get my haircut. She then proceeded to go off on a long rant about how 'difficult' it was to cut curly hair, tried to explain to me how it needed to be cut (after 26 years of living apparently I don't know how my own hair needs to be cut) and that she couldn't possibly touch my hair because of all the different ways, she wouldn't know which is the right way to do it. This was then followed by the lady doing my nails and the hairdresser ranting about Meghan Markle being aggressive, and an attention seeker, and a gold digger. Safe to say I did not go back there.

"For centuries Blacks and Women have not defined these standards. We straighten our hair with heat and chemicals to meet those Eurocentric standards. For too many years there have been too many cases of employees being denied a promotion or even being fired because of the way they chose to wear their hair."(Senator Holly J. Mitchell)

The question arises: why should people's hair be classified as "unprofessional"?
Over the past decades, there have been numerous reports that Black women have been discriminated against as "unprofessional" in the workplace because of their natural Afro hair or braids-like hairstyles.

In 2015, Bournemouth University graduate Lara Odoffin received this email after an interview in which a job offer was revoked:

"Unfortunately we cannot accept braids - it is simply part of the uniform and grooming requirements we get from our clients. If you are unable to take them out I unfortunately won't be able to offer you any work".

Her braids were apparently not "suitable" for selling high-quality products. This is the association that some organisations and people have that Black hairstyles = unprofessional. That Black hairstyles **do not** equal high quality. How can something that can take days of hard work, be regarded as unprofessional or low-quality?

In 2016, an employer at a London Harrods high fashion department store, targeted Black employees and demanded that their hair be chemically straightened. While these events are primarily about hair, the motivations behind these actions are linked to racial marginalisation, including discrimination based on cultural characteristics and physical features such as skin colour and hair.

Parmer (2004) states that physical beauty is a very important factor as it influences social relationships, choice of friends and career opportunities. For women, the beauty hierarchy prioritises straight, long, and preferably blonde hair, as well as fair skin and light eyes. Women with these traits or who meet these standards are traditionally said to be attractive. Although hair is a symbol of women's beauty, this hierarchy views curly and Afro hair as "unprocessed" or "ugly" and therefore unsuitable for many social contexts in which "traditional beauty" prevails. Of course, the problem is not just having or wanting long straight hair, but a system that bases a woman's value on her beauty first and uses one type of beauty as a reference.

It must be recognised that the "hair dilemma" - the problem of the hairstyle - for Black women is not just in its own right, but is linked to race issues as well as gender. On the issue of racism, beauty ideals see Black women as less attractive because their appearance is incompatible with the beauty given to fair skin, a thin nose and straight hair that are part of the Caucasian aesthetic. In addition, they are often referred to as "tough" or "masculine" because they are usually attributed to the characteristics of men, which is why it is called "defeminisation" of black women.

These definitions and considerations have a strong impact on the employment opportunities reserved for them. In 2019, a Dove brand study reported that Black women were 80% more likely than white women to modify their natural hair to meet social norms or expectations in the workplace. In addition, the study states that 50% said that their employer sent them home for their hair or that they knew at least one Black woman who had received such treatment. In fact, many feel compelled to find alternatives that are considered professional. It is also important to note that many women choose these options for fashion, convenience or other personal preferences, without external causes or feelings of inferiority.

Unfortunately, stories like the ones listed above don't just happen in the workplace. In fact, many women experience discrimination from an early age. In 2018, the case of Ruby Williams, the repeated expulsion of a young English girl from her East London school, caused a stir as her Afro hair was "too big". There are also other cases of schools in Jamaica and South Africa banning the use of afro hairstyles for students. These messages are very damaging to young people's self-esteem and body image. It is not difficult to find chemical hair straighteners for Black girls who receive regular treatments from a young age to look "cleaner".

While Rapunzel, Cinderella, Sleeping Beauty and Barbie are definitely part of the reality for White girls, Black girls are taught that "White beauty" means happiness. Extra manipulation such as hair breakage, as well as skin pain can result from excessive and direct manipulation of curls. They also take longer to grow as follicles usually stay longer in the telogen phase - the relaxation phase. By using methods like braids, curls, types and knots, known hairstyles are not only fashionable, but also help to keep hair healthy and strong.

In 2023, Disney released a live-action of The Little Mermaid with Halle Bailey playing Ariel. My own niece commented in the cinema that we looked like her and she could be our older sister (it also made me smile that she thought a 23 year old could be my older sister, bless her). The amount of hate across social media platforms for Halle and also Disney for casting her, comments that red heads still need representation (she still had red hair in the film) in the original she was White now people can't relate because **this** little mermaid is Black (those old films still exist and now more people can relate to Ariel) as well as the film literally being set in the caribbean sea.

Going back in time, Afro hair has a very rich history. Clothing and ornaments originated in Africa, varying across cultures and countries and often reflecting important social and religious meanings for communities. During the slave trade across the globe, women hid seeds, rice and pulses in beads - a series of braids tied along the head. This type of braid was also used as a real escape card from the plantations. In the United States, with the Black Power movement of the 1950s, the famous Afro hairstyle of African-American activists known as "The Natural" became part of Black pride - and associated with the political changes of the time.

In December 2017, ELLE magazine released a documentary entitled Braided: An American Hair Story on their YouTube platform, featuring actress Lupita Nyong'o, writer Ayana Byrd, and other celebrities and original stylists. The documentary tackles the issue of the adoption of African hairstyles in the mainstream media and among non-black celebrities like reality TV character Kim Kardashian West. When a non-Black person wears hairstyles of African origin, the style is viewed as a fashion accessory since the individual experiences the hairstyle in the context of White privilege - racial privilege.

Here comes the concept of cultural appropriation - cultural appropriation when the ways and habits of particular communities become part of a common culture as consumed as "products". The video shows the perceived disdain for "bleaching" many Black hairstyles. One example is cornrow braids, renamed to the media "Kim Kardashian braids" or "boxer braids" after Kim Kardashian West and UFC fighters made them popular among non - Black groups. However, the use of afro hairstyles by black women is still a source of discrimination. In contrast, when a black woman changes her appearance to be seen as "respectful" or "smart", she is still and always seen as a black woman.

In recent years, there has been an increase in the number of Black women who are starting to feel free to choose their style and who are opting for straight hair or traditional African hairstyles to feel so beautiful and so professional. Afro hairstyles are now embraced by many Black women, including successful and highly skilled people, who choose to show off their natural beauty, inspire confidence, and go against the norm, whether intentionally or not. In addition, a decrease in the use of chemical extensions has been attributed to awareness of the negative consequences of these treatments and some influential social media and YouTube videos showing various ways to care for Afro-natural hair.

But let it be noted, Michelle Obama opted to have the usually same straight hairstyle during her husband's presidency, so the news never reported on her hair, or changin hair. It's only been since she is no longer FLOTUS, that she has embraced natural hair styles. She knew what the media and public perception would be like - if she had worked natural hair styles during those 8 years.

When it comes to going into a work setting, you need to do whatever you are comfortable with. If you'd rather have straight hair - don't shame yourself for that. But don't let someone or a company force you into doing or presenting yourself in a way that isn't right for you.

I straightened my hair for every job interview I had for years, I was so scared of people judging me for my hair and it would be part of the reason I did not get a job. It's only been in the last few years that I came to the decision of "I will present myself in my true form, and if they don't like it, I don't want to work there anyway".

Looking the Part

It doesn't stop at your hairstyle though. Your outfit needs to look the part too. Some places you work will have a uniform (hurrah) you won't have to think about what to wear. But there will be some businesses that require a casual, business casual or formal business look. Now whilst I've written this book to help you prepare for the instances of discrimination you may face in the workplace, I always want to help you in general when it comes to embarking on your career.

So I've listed a number of different outfit ideas for you to give you some inspiration when dressing for an interview or when going into work.

TIP: For your interview, dress one stage smarter than their usual work attire.

Completely relaxed (tracksuits, hoodies)
Casual (leggings, jumpers)
Smart Casual (jeans, shirts)
Business Casual (trousers, shirts)
Formal Business (pantsuits, blazers)

When you first join a company, you need to know how to dress appropriately for each situation. Is there every day office where a different 'level' of smart than if you're out at an event representing the company? How about if you have a team-building day?

What you wear to a job interview or jobs fair, is likely to be different from your everyday work attire. If you are a business owner, talk to your employees about what to expect in terms of the type of clothing that should be worn at work. Most companies provide dress code guidelines to their employees to provide guidance on the types of clothing that are allowed and prohibited on business and leisure days.

It's worth noting that if you were clothing that you would identify as part of your culture as part of your everyday wear, and would wear to work - it's possible your workplace could deem this as inappropriate. This comes from a lack of education and understanding about your clothing. In this situation, I suggest you go to work wearing what you want and nobody says anything then great, but if you're pulled aside, explain the cultural context of your outfit, and then get it in writing to protect yourself. If your boss or manager says you can't wear it - get them to explain in an email. They are discriminating against you and your culture.

If your company has a casual dress code, they need to communicate what is acceptable to the staff. Casual does not mean sloppy or mismatched clothing. Avoid clothes that are overly exposed or abusive.

Diversity is having a seat at the table, inclusion is having a voice, and belonging is having that voice be heard.

~ Liz Fosslien

Going the Extra Mile

Ever heard one of these statements before?

"You're so smart.. for a Black person."
"For a Black girl, you sure are beautiful."
"Wow, your English is really good."
"I didn't know you were able to do something like that."

I hope you haven't. And if you have - I'm sorry. There has been a presumption for a long time that Black people can't be skilled, beautiful, intelligent or more. Some people may not mean offence when they make these comments, but of course the recipient of them will be offended. Why wouldn't they be?!

Because of these ingrained opinions that have been passed down for generations, we have to go the extra mile. It's not fair, and it's not right. But as explained before, the more of ethnic minorities that go the extra mile, and get the platform to make change will pave the way for others taking on these journeys later down the line. This means that as an ethnic minority, you will need to put in ten times the amount of work to achieve the same recognition, the same promotions. So double that, to get the job and get the promotions.

For many, working in the midst of a global pandemic has not been easy. For those of us who have been fortunate enough to be able to continue working from home, it has still been necessary to make ourselves presentable for non-stop virtual meetings, and to learn to be productive as the boundaries between our personal and professional lives continue to blur.

We're running out of good series to stream, Instagram lives to watch, recipes to cook. We feel lost and we are afraid. We don't know when this will all be over. But there is the story of two confinements. Because while some have been enchanted by banana bread recipes, others have had to manage to survive a pandemic in a country where they were not supposed to live.

Over the past few years, Black people have not only watched their friends and family members die of the coronavirus at an accelerating rate (more so than their White counterparts), but they have also seen people who look like them being shot as they go jogging, being murdered in their own homes, threatened while birdwatching, and ruthlessly asphyxiated in front of the cameras. And yet, day after day, we get out of bed, we answer our emails. We show up with a smile and put our pain and fears aside. We swallow our anger by responding to our bosses, offering our help, and working twice as hard for half as much and that's all we've always been doing. But here's a scoop for any White people who haven't already guessed: your Black co-workers may look fine right now, but chances are it isn't the case.

The likelihood that your Black colleague has lost a family member to Covid-19 is painfully high. The likelihood that your Black colleague has been traumatised by Amy Cooper's viral video of a White woman using skin colour and the privileges that come with it to threaten a Black man. The likelihood that your Black co-worker will be scared to go for a run, or terrified when her husband leaves home, or just be enraged by the endless lies the world keeps telling us about equality freedoms is so high that you will need a ladder to get down.

A hearing held in June 2023 showed that a Dorset Police Officer was sacked over discriminatory, sexist and offensive messages shared in a police WhatsApp group. A person in a position of power. All you need to do is Google search 'Police Officer fired' for a whole host of terrifying offences that have happened to your colleague, your neighbour, an old school friend - because of the colour of our skin.

And yet, this person responded to your passive, aggressive email, and kept smiling when you asked condescending questions. Or she found the strength to get out of bed and just show up. Everyday, Black people take the personal trauma that we all know to be true and put it aside to protect White people who are unaware that it is almost impossible to go on living when the world is built this way. It's hard to be at your best when you see White women feigning terror on the phone with the police in the hope that the police will arrest and maybe kill a Black man. It's even harder to watch these cops kill this Black man on video, but we're still going to work. We swallow our rage, our tears, our fear and our sadness. Messages are exchanged in discussion groups. We send articles that reflect our feelings. We publish, repost and retweet on social networks. But we don't take our pain to work.

So, even as you face this pandemic that has ravaged our way of life – and which has claimed the lives of so many people prematurely, regardless of their ethnicity – recognise the burden that falls disproportionately on your colleagues. And know that they will never show it. And while we've been told that degrees, jobs, and accomplishments will somehow protect us from being treated like second-class citizens; although we were led to believe that working hard and being an active member of society meant society would treat us like human beings, we learned the painful truth - it's not.

Black students have been told in the past that they can only excel if they are "twice as good" as other (White) students. This does not allow them to make mistakes: small mistakes make big mistakes and, when summarised, can ruin even small possibilities. It is not an ideal case for a Black student. That said, it is not surprising that it is directly in line with the systemic racism and oppression that has affected people of colour since inception.

This goes back to the 1954 case of Brown v. Board of Education, a landmark Supreme Court decision that helped encourage universities to admit more Black students and end segregation. Since the early days of MSU (Michigan State University), the university has sought to position itself on the right side of humanity by promoting racial integration: in 1907, MSU awarded its first degree to a Black man, John Somerville. Opening the doors for Black students to try to get into big universities, by setting precedents and by abolishing racist politics, helped to foster a sense (still underestimated) that they deserved to be in them. Of course, this advancement in social justice does not alleviate the stereotypical pressure and threat that often accompanies navigating these classes and often dealing with micro-aggression as a Black student, from the conspicuous wonder of the professor to their own confession in doubt about one's own ability.

When Black students can do honours or crash courses in high school, they are already prepared to do better than others who are privileged to do less work and benefit from it. A Black student will often do their best to avoid the ridicule and discrimination they may face.

In the USC 2020 Student Demographics Report, of the 46,000 students who attend college, only 5.5% were black. This clearly shows that there is still much room for improvement in recruiting students from under-represented communities. Furthermore, it cannot be said that Black students are not obliged to overcompensate in the hope of acceptance: it is the responsibility of institutions to correct the systemic discrimination in its own structure.

What makes things worse is that the same students will one day leave their universities, with degrees in hand, ready to face the uncertain world of work that awaits them. So many of these students will see the concept of double time and double effort emerge and continue in professional life despite their obvious qualities. They are constantly reminded that other applicants for the same job may be under-qualified but receive the job because of their race. This reinforces the fact that Black applicants have to go through a more rigorous process in order to be recognised by the selected employer.

Harvard Business School conducted a study to examine how applicants from marginalised communities "clarify" their resumes, leaving information such as hobbies, names, and membership of organisations that would assign them directly to race specifically to prevent them from returning for an interview. 25% of Black applicants who made light of their resumes were recalled, compared to 10% of those who provided information suggesting they were from an under-represented community. It is absurd that such a candidate would have to omit certain details in order to increase their chances of getting a job - this is clear and serious racism that perpetuates the misconception that minority candidates should deny their identity in order to forward.

Not to mention the added stress and frustration of being a Black student and always remembering that the only way to get and keep an opportunity is to always do your best and do everything when possible - consuming and debilitating. White people do not have to deal with these internal struggles as they have no reason to believe that their efforts or contribution will be manifested in an unusual way. The hard work of putting Black students on the scales alone does not eliminate these stereotypes, but perpetuates them. With this in mind, it is vital that workplaces and schools continue to build on their work to recognize the inherent bias and discrimination in these systems. These institutions, which must work actively to mitigate these consequences, must have unlearned stereotypes, and the black students involved, who should never feel compelled to challenge themselves beyond their means. may be done by a qualified candidate or student.

As the world continues the difficult dialogue on racism, a conversation that has been put back in the spotlight following the police killings of Breonna Taylor, George Floyd and many others, is about to tackle systemic racism, which is interfering with that it crosses education and work. Fairness and equality can only be expected to be the most important (and unique) factors in assessing the qualifications of a black student and this will interfere with his or her professional career. Recognition as a qualified person to break racial prejudice should never be the norm and it is essential that all schools and workplaces take steps to ensure that this does not happen again.

So in light of all of these, how can you go the extra mile? What can you do to stand out during your interview process?

- Discuss what is expected from you and be honest about your skills, and discuss what you will expect from the company.
- Talk about your career plan, where do you see yourself in five years? Show that you see yourself being at the company for the long term.
- Ask the employer questions that will add value to yourself , these should show your understanding of the company and the role itself.
- After your interview, send them feedback. Let them know how you think it went, keep it positive and personable.
- Ask for the next steps, when can you expect to hear from them? Should you do anything to help with your application?
- Show you will start making an impact from your first day, go in with ideas that align with the businesses values and goals.
- Demonstrate how you will fit in with the team. Not just because you will do your workload and support them, but socially too. Show you are great with a full range of people.
- Get the right time slot. Avoid the Monday slog and the Friday wishing for the weekend moment.

Straight after lunch they may be in a food coma, early morning they're still waking up, right before lunch - they're fantasising about what food to pick! Tuesday, Wednesday and Thursday mid-morning are the best slots.
- Practise how you get to the interview and where you're parking beforehand. On the same day at the same time the week before. This will reduce your anxiety on the day because you already know where you are going. Don't arrive more than ten minutes early to the interview.
- Keep back ups. Your CV, your presentation, your cover letter. Keep a copy in physical print, on a USB and on the desktop on your laptop. Don't be caught unprepared!

By following this list, you're giving yourself a head start on getting the job, or getting the promotion.

Writing Your CV

The best head start you can give yourself is at the very first hurdle. The application process. What do you need in order to be invited into an interview? A cracking CV. There are many platforms now such as Indeed and Reed where you will enter all your information and it will send employers a 'typical' CV template, but for those jobs that don't advertise this way - you will need to send in your own CV.

My first tip is to have two versions that include the same information but look slightly different. A PDF version that looks pretty, and a word document version in case they are unable to open the PDF. Canva is a great online tool you can use (for free) to create your PDF version. Google docs/word will be perfect for your secondary version.

You want to save the design for last, the first thing you need to do is start writing. Your first draft is likely to be fairly long, as you work out what information is most important to include, but by the time you finish it should be no longer than a page.

The essential information you should be including is;
Your name
The title of the job you are applying for
An introduction to yourself
Your contact details (number, email, LinkedIn)
Your top seven skills

Your education history
Your last 1 - 3 roles/education in detail
Your experience continued

All of this information NEEDS to be tailored for the job you are applying for. I know it feels long winded to change it up every time, but this will give you a greater chance at getting to the interview stage, they will see you have tailored it. Most people do feel lazy about this - so here is your first chance to stand out.

Introduction to yourself
This needs to be a fairly short paragraph that highlights your strengths and experience, showing your personality and keeps their attention. It's important here to include how many years experience you have in the industry for the role that you are applying for, or if it is your first role then how you have been interested in this industry. This is a good place to note down your strengths. Take a look at the job description and any of the skills they deem as 'desirable' (that you have) would be great to add in here.

TOP TIP: Search the job role and company in LinkedIn to find somebody who does it now/has done it previously. What does it say in their job description for this role? What can you take from that and add into your resume?

Make sure that you make it clear in this section that you do have a personal passion for the role that you are applying for. You don't want this just because it's a job and it will pay the bills (though this may be the reason, and that's okay, companies just don't like to hear this) make it clear you see this as a career opportunity and you can see yourself at the company for a long time.

Also, don't use any words or examples you don't understand. If you get questioned on this during your interview, you don't want to stumble on something that you wrote yourself.

Example: I've worked within Events & Communications spaces for over five years and it's something I genuinely enjoy and take great pride in. My experience gained from working within multiple industries (most notably my Digital Agency experience) has allowed me to become extremely adaptable, as well as adopt unique skills, but mainly it's my attention to detail, conscientiousness and data-oriented approach to delivering tailored messaging to ensure the communications that are delivered are with maximum impact.

Your contact details
The three most important things to include here are your contact number, email address and a link to your LinkedIn profile. Your number and email are self explanatory, but your LinkedIn profile needs to be a copy and paste of your CV, with much more detail.

I've included some LinkedIn profiles below for you to take a look at.

https://www.linkedin.com/in/meganwellman/
https://www.linkedin.com/in/danielleantoinette/
https://www.linkedin.com/in/jermainelmurray/
https://www.linkedin.com/in/shannon-tribaja/

Your top seven skills
According to resume genius, you should list four to ten skills on your CV. I personally recommend seven as the sweet spot. This is another time when you should get up the description for the role that you are applying for - what skills are they looking for? They likely have over seven so you won't be able to include them all, but you need a good mix of skills they say are essential, desirable, as well as your strengths.

DO NOT write down anything you have no experience in. Whilst it is common for people to exaggerate on their CV, and this is fine, do not write down anything you are not capable of doing. If this is discovered during your interview process, you may feel embarrassed and risk the job offer. If this is discovered after you have been offered a job, you may lose your position for misleading.

Your education history
Some people go really overboard here when they don't need to. Your future employer will not care that you were on the school council in Year 4. You need to keep this section brief and to the point. Start it off with your most

recent qualifications and go back until you think when relevant.

I really recommend doing a short online course relevant to the job that you are applying for. You can find these online for free or for a small cost of normally under £30. This will help you stand out from the crowd as you're showing a dedication to the industry and you've taken your own time to further your knowledge on the subject.

When I was leaving college and trying to start my career in the events/marketing industry at 17, I applied to an apprenticeship for a technology company. My boss told me after I accepted the role that the fact I had done an online events course a few months before, had really helped set me apart from other candidates.

Your last 1-3 roles/education in detail
What you are writing here depends on whether this is the first job you are applying for, if it's the first career-orientated job you are applying for, or if it's your second career role.

Your experience is going to heavily dictate how much you are able to write. If this is your first ever job, this is when you need to expand on your education much more. What skills have you learned and developed throughout your journey to stay in education? You need to demonstrate that your transition to the working world won't be a difficult one, you're used to the routine, working hard and are adaptable.

If you've already had a job and you're looking to move into something that focuses more on your career, you have a little more 'life-work experience' to work with. This is where you can show how transferable your skills are. For example, if you have been working as a Retail Assistant for a supermarket and now you are applying for a Junior Software Developer role, you could say; 'When working as a Retail Assistant, I had to assist all sorts of customers during a really difficult time whilst there was a pandemic. I was dealing with customers who were dealing with grievances, were irritable and panicky or who were really lovely. As your junior software developer, I'll be able to speak to all levels of staff from my team, to yourself, my manager and the leadership team, tailoring my approach to each colleague.'

On the assumption that this role is your second role in the industry, you will find it slightly easier to tailor your CV to suit. When writing the job description for the role you are currently undertaking, you will know what they are looking for in the role that you are applying for. This is where you can slightly alter responsibilities you currently have to closer match the role you are applying for. Slight exaggeration is okay here, but nothing you won't be able to explain.

You will need to make sure you include your top responsibilities from the role that you have been doing. It won't be possible to include everything that you do on a day to day basis, so it's essential you know how to include all the important bits. For example, if you need to share pieces of content you have created, you can list it like so;

Content creation: writing articles, case studies, website content, monthly newsletters, email campaigns & awards submissions (3 shortlisted, 1 honourable mention, 1 win).

This allows you to go into detail without the need to create a different bullet point for every piece of content you are able to create. There's enough examples to show you are well versed in this skill, and adding in an ROI (the awards results) shows you are good at what you do.

Your experience continued
You may not have enough space to include all of your experience, and you don't want to let your CV go over one page long. It needs to be short to keep the hiring manager's attention. They may have hundreds of CVs to sift through.

You just need to list here dates, job titles, companies and make a note that references are available on request. You can discuss anything worth noting in your interview that may be missed in this section, if it is relevant to the role you are applying for.

People who can provide a reference for you will be previous employers, professors, teachers or professionals. For example, one of your parents' friends who runs their own business could provide a character reference for you.

PDF vs Word Document
If you can, apply with the PDF version of your CV. You can make this much more visually appealing and use the company's brand colours on your CV.

You won't always be able to do this, for example if they use Indeed/Reed or an online system to take job applications. This is why you need a word document version to copy and paste your information easily over, or apply with the word document if for some example they can't use the PDF on their end.

Cover Letter Tips

Not every employer is going to ask for a cover letter, but you should always include one. It does not have to be exceptionally long, and when they don't ask for one, you can send a fairly short one. Just be sure to include the name of the role you are applying for, your top skills, why you're applying and if there is anything else you can do to support your application. A rough template to follow could be;

"Dear [Sir/Madam/Hiring Manager's name if you know]

Please find attached my [CV/Indeed CV/Reed CV] as an application for the role of [Job title]. I believe my [Skill 1], [Skill 2] and [Skill 3] skills and experience in the [Relevant] industry as well as my passion to succeed will make me a real asset to the team at [Company name].

I love your passion for [Information found online] and it's something I really resonate with. If there is anything else I can do for you to support my application, please let me know.

Thank you for the opportunity to apply, and I look forward to hearing from you.

Kind regards,
[Your name]"

This is short, snappy and will get their attention. You are clearly highlighting some of your top skills (check the job description for ones to include) whilst making it personal to the company. You've clearly done your research and have shown you are already dedicated by asking if there is anything else you can do.

When companies ask for a long cover letter, whilst normally unnecessary, it's because they want you to talk about how you think you will fit into the company, why you want to work for them, what you can do for them and what sets you apart from the competition.

Fitting into the company; check the company website and social media. This is where they will be sharing what the culture of the company is. You need to share here how you think you will be a culture fit. Do they have frequent team outings? Talk about how much you love being part of a team and how important it is to build relationships with your colleagues. Their socials will give you a good idea on what the culture is like.

Why do you want to work for them; this is where you need to do what may feel like a little bit of sucking up. You want to explain that this is an opportunity that you don't want to miss. Check the website for what they outline as their core values/mission statement. Be sure to include these as part of the reason why you want to work for this particular company. Include that you think you can see yourself at this company for a long period of time.

What can you do for them; use the job description to help you with this section. Pick out the few things you know you can do and that you're good at. Use ROI's from your current role to show you've got the work to back up what you're saying too. This is a good time to say that you are adaptable, can support other departments during busier periods, and are always looking to further your knowledge. Being adaptable is a highly sought-after skill. Explain your dedication, passion and need to go above and beyond.

What sets you apart from the competition; this is the trickier one. You never know what somebody else is going to put. So this is where you do need to try and find something personal about yourself that really will set you apart from the competition. This needs to be more about a problem you can solve for the company (the solution) rather than the product you are offering (your experience and skills.) If you really struggle to come up with something, ask your colleagues/friends/classmates what makes you special and/or different.

A couple of ideas you can start with (but still need to personalise) could be;
- Mention what you did to go the extra mile during the interview process (did you do an online course relevant to the role?)
- Is there anything you do in your spare time that is relevant to the role you are applying for?

- Has the company shared some recent news that you can relate to?
- Do you have an example of something that you have previously achieved that is a solution to a problem they are trying to solve?
- Have you worked on similar projects so know what problems are likely to arise? You can explain how this will save the team time and energy to focus on high value tasks
- Engage the reader: how to start your letter; Once upon a time, it was normal to write "For the attention / CA of whomever you are responsible for", "Dear Sir" or "Dear Madam, Dear Sir" in the opening formula of the cover letter. But times have changed.

Today's job search is largely based on establishing an interpersonal emotional connection. Always try to address your letter to a specific person. If the hiring manager's name is not mentioned in the job posting, do some research and, if necessary, make a call to find out who you need to contact to get the job you aspire to. According to some psychological studies, people like to have their name written, which makes them more likely to sit in front of your letter and pay attention.

Additionally, a letter addressed to a single person is more likely to receive a response than a letter sent to an entire department. Sometimes, the hiring manager's name may not be disclosed on purpose; in this case, being tactful might be the winning strategy: opt for "To the kind attention of the hiring manager" or "To the kind attention of the hiring team of (company name)".

- Cover letter body: the right style. The next challenge is to write the body of the letter: 1 page / 400 words maximum, divided into paragraphs. Write with your goal in mind: to convince the hiring manager that you are the ideal candidate. But before we venture into the content of each paragraph, let's talk for a moment about their visual impact.

    Font choice is an important factor in the readability of your cover letter: some job potentials might be fine with fonts such as Times New Roman, but most modern companies prefer visually smoother, "cleaner" fonts - such as Arial, Verdana and Helvetica. Calibri even replaced Times New Roman as the default font in Microsoft Word, which says a lot. For your cover letter, therefore, choose a modern and easy-to-read font: nothing too flashy or elaborate, nothing that draws attention to itself.

    After all, you want the reader's attention to be on your text, not the font you used. Go for a font size between 10 and 12 points: below 10 points the font is in fact difficult to read, but if you go above 12 your letter will start to look like a children's book.

Left Align Text: This style is known as "flag" alignment, as the effect of lines of text of different lengths is that of a waving flag. We do not recommend justifying the text from margin to margin: you will end up with a page divided into blocks of text in which the words are stretched horizontally to reach the margin or in which there is an excess of "holes", gruyere effect.

- Write an irrepressible introduction
In the opening paragraph of your cover letter, you need to be able to 'sell your case' concisely and persuasively. In the first paragraph of your letter, you need to find a way to: introduce yourself briefly, identify the position you are applying for, and start hinting that you are more than qualified for the job. Get the right tone of voice right from the start: friendly, enthusiastic, confident, and competent - without being arrogant or conceited. Make your introduction catch the reader's attention, but for the right reasons.

Simply put, the opening paragraph is your chance to make a good first impression and give your reader a reason to keep reading.

- Show your persuasiveness in the body of the letter

  The body of your cover letter is where you need to convince your reader that you are the ideal candidate for the position. Don't be afraid to brag a little: if you don't promote your candidacy, who has to do it?

  Talk about your work experience and be specific when it comes to mentioning career milestones and workplace achievements. Where possible, use facts and figures (numbers, amounts, percentages) to quantify your results and your work history. For example, go beyond the boundaries of your resume and tell about a time when you promptly addressed and solved a problem.

  A question we often see is: Can bulleted lists be used in a cover letter? The short answer is: yes. The slightly longer answer is: use them sparingly, evaluating whether they actually benefit the appearance and readability of your letter. Avoid turning your cover letter into a second resume, defeating its purpose.

  In the body of the letter you can also mention relevant educational goals, certifications and skills. Additionally, you can choose to share your aspirations for the future, particularly in relation to the position you are applying for. Make sure you study the job description carefully and show that you meet all the necessary requirements. But be warned: While mirroring the terminology used in the job posting may be to your advantage, make sure you are always honest. In fact, during the interview, you will be asked to further explain your goals and your skills, and all the knots will come to a head.

The tone of your writing is also important. To ensure that your writing, the values highlighted and the level of formality are in line with those of the company you are applying to, be sure to check their social media, website, any interviews with managerial staff or otherwise material available online.

- Concluding paragraph and salutation
Your closing paragraph can include a summary, thank you, or anything else important that you haven't had a chance to say yet. Once you've finished your letter, be sure to choose an appropriate greeting: "Sincerely", "Kindest", "Sincerely".

Don't forget to show clear interest in getting back in touch - let your potential employer know that you'd be happy to interview in person or over the phone. You could also add that you are always reachable via the contact information provided in the header (some sources suggest repeating your phone number and email address in the concluding paragraph).

Make sure there is no doubt that you are seriously interested in the position, that you are eager to get back to you and that you are ready for the next step.

Make sure you reread and proofread your letter carefully - ideally, ask someone else to take a look at it. Any grammatical and typing errors are in fact among the main reasons why cover letters and curriculum vitae are discarded.

Interview Tips

From the moment you accept the invite to interview, you are being judged on how well you will perform in this role and fit in with the company. Use what you learnt from the chapters 'Looking the part' and 'Professional hairstyles' to ensure you turn up looking the best you can.

To obtain a job or internship position it is essential to face at least one job interview. The meeting is a real opportunity, not only for the candidate but also for the recruiter, through which a positive exchange of information takes place. Through the interview, in fact, the recruiter acquires details about the candidate who, in turn, can receive more information about the company and the open position for which you've presented yourself. Therefore, it is very important for you to understand how to prepare yourself for a job interview, focusing on previous experiences, on your training, on the skills you have acquired, and on soft skills .

Essentials to take to your interview are;
- Water, so you do not get a dry throat when you are talking and in case they do not offer you a drink
- Hairbrush and hair bands, if it has been windy you want to be able to tidy yourself up before meeting the hiring manager

- Tissue, you don't know how the temperature change from outside to inside may be, you don't want to keep sniffing in your interview! Keep a tissue on you in case you need to blow your nose
- Snack, if you have been nervous and were unable to eat before you left, you don't want an awkward tummy rumble
- CV, hard copy, on your laptop and on a USB. You need to find it easy to refer to your experience. It's not a memory test it's okay to have notes
- Interview prep, have it in the same format as above. You should also have a blank pad and pen for when they answer your questions

Before your interview, do a practice run of turning up. Work out how you are going to get there, how long you need to get ready that day and where you are going to park, or how far the walk is from the bus stop to the head office. You should aim to be in the area at least half an hour before your interview start time. This is to allow time for traffic accidents, unforeseen circumstances and more. On the actual day, you want to walk into the head office five to ten minutes before your interview is due to start. They are likely to have a few interviews that day, so you don't want to irritate them by turning up too early, or being late and messing up their schedule for the day.

You'll need to arrive prepared first, so here are some tips to prepare for an interview:

1. Look for information: studying is very important to prepare for a job interview. Search online for information about the company and the services or products it offers and carefully review the job description, in this way you will demonstrate your real interest in the position. You can also study the recruiter's LinkedIn profile.

2. Keep an eye on your social profiles: adjust your profiles, set your privacy options correctly and update your LinkedIn profile so that it is complete.

3. Practice: Be prepared to deal with the questions, by doing some tests in front of the mirror or with someone willing to help you. Get ready to introduce yourself, to tell about your skills and experiences. Remember to also prepare some questions to ask the recruiter to demonstrate your interest.

4. Focus on the interview: don't get distracted! Do not make important commitments in the days before or after the job interview to be able to concentrate as much as possible on the interview. Keep your phone away during the interview - even when you're in the waiting area.

5. Rest and eat well: get a good night's sleep before the interview, to arrive rested.
Nutrition is also important, carbohydrates are a good source of energy to avoid sugar drops and stay focused.

When the hiring manager comes to greet you, maintain eye contact and offer a strong handshake. Keep an open face and smile when appropriate. Keep your body language open throughout the interview - don't cross your arms. Legs resting on crossed legs is a good go to, and when talking using your hands to gesture is engaging. If they offer you a drink, accept it. They will likely have one too and this shows that you are comfortable with them. If they give you options of tea/coffee/water, go for the water. The caffeine in tea and coffee can have a bad effect on you.

The next part will be when they are asking you questions. Try to keep it conversational. Ask them questions throughout if they flow nicely with the current topic. The first question 99% of the time will be 'So, tell me about yourself?' This is the time to sell yourself, show your personality and find common ground with the interviewer. Make sure you have done a LinkedIn/Facebook/Instagram stalk beforehand so you can find a bond with them. Don't make it exceptionally obvious - if they won a Baton Twirling competition when they were six, don't bring this up. More along the lines of if they have a pet dog, if they post frequent pictures of them playing tennis for fun, if they're a foodie etc.

Here are some tips for controlling non-verbal communication:
- Always introduce yourself with a smile.

- If the interview is taking place in the company, don't sit down before the recruiter . If you are already seated and waiting for them, get up when they arrive.
- Avoid playing with your hands or nervously moving your feet. Sit in a composed and "open" way, for example instead of standing with folded arms you can try to rest your hands on the table.
- Maintain eye contact with the recruiter, even in times of difficulty. In this way you will communicate safety and will not let the discomfort leak out. Show constant interest in what you are told, through nods and pertinent questions.
- Follow all of the previous tips, but try to be natural - taking the right attitudes awkwardly can be really counterproductive.

Group interview: how to behave
Sometimes companies adopt the method of selecting the group interview, in order to evaluate the communication and interpersonal skills of the candidates, but also the attitudes to leadership and mediation.

Here are some tips to follow to face the group interview :
- As with normal interviews, the first rule is punctuality.
- Suitable clothing.
- Pay attention to non-verbal communication, so as not to let the agitation shine through.

- Prepare a self -presentation : it is generally required, for a duration of a few minutes.
- Be proactive, to leave a good impression on the recruiter you need to demonstrate the ability to take control of the situation. For example, come in first if no one comes forward at the start of the interview.
- If the recruiter proposes a role play, try to keep consistency with the role and situation that are assigned to you.
- Be sure of yourself, but accept the ideas of others to avoid confrontation, thus demonstrating openness and the ability to mediate and moderate.

The remote job interview
The job market is increasingly globalised and, thanks to technology, has acquired new tools to connect candidates and recruiters.The pandemic has undoubtedly also had its weight and remote interviews are increasingly widespread, using applications such as Skype, Zoom, Teams or Google Meet. Despite its telematic nature, the interview in Skype or with another remote application has the same value as a traditional job interview , thus deserving the same preparation.

Here's how to get prepared:
- Choose a professional nickname . The ideal would be to use your name and surname (for example with the formula "name.surname"). Even the profile photo must correspond to the

requirements of seriousness and professionalism.
- It is advisable to reserve an account for job interviews, in order to avoid inappropriate interruptions from online friends.
- Do an audio / video test before starting: check that the webcam, microphone and connection are working.
- Set up the webcam and choose the most appropriate shot: opt for a neutral background and lighting that makes the face clearly visible .
- Take care of your image , even if you won't face the interview in person: dress professionally and completely (not just the part that will appear on video).
- Even for a Skype appointment, punctuality is essential. Also, try to avoid distractions, put your phone in a different room and make sure you are not disturbed by anyone who lives in the house with you.
- During the interview, look carefully at the recruiter, avoiding staring at a point in the room or looking at the picture in the window.
- You won't have a handshake to greet and thank the recruiter. Do not say "bye bye" with your hand, simply thank and politely greet your interlocutor in a formal and professional way .

Not just answers: what questions to ask at a job interview?

The interview, as we have said, is an important opportunity for exchange, through which you can acquire more information on the job offered and on the company. For this reason, it is very important to remember to ask the recruiter a few questions, showing interest in the position and work environment. Remember that it is best to avoid questions about holidays and working hours, at least during the first interview.

Here are some questions you can ask, depending on the circumstances:
- What sets your company apart from your competitors?
- What's your personal favourite thing about working for this company?
- What is the company's strongest/best selling product?
- Is there anything about my skills or experience that would make you hesitate to offer me this role? (This gives you the chance to address it there and then, and not leave the interview with any questions hanging over the hiring managers head)
- I'd love to know how the company supported their employees during the Black Lives Matter protests in June 2020?

- Do you have many employees of an ethnic minority? How do you support them?
- Do you have a transparent wage policy?
- What will the first few weeks or so look like for me whilst I'm getting up to speed on everything?
- How do you determine success in this role?
- When would you like me to start?

TOP TIP: When the interviewer asks what your salary expectations are, respond with 'I'd love to understand how your company values this role. What is your budget?' This allows you to know the range they are expecting to pay before giving a number out yourself. If you're comfortable sharing a salary with the company, I'd recommend a range. For example, if you know you want £23,000 per annum, suggest the range to them of £23,000 - £28,000. You can say something like;

"The salary range I am looking for is £23,000 - £26,000. Once we've completed the interview process, and if you came to the decision you'd like to hire me, I'd love you to offer me what you think is right based on my skills and experience that I have demonstrated to you."

This stops one figure being put on your head, so if they are comparing you to other candidates, if one is the exact same level as you and they said £24k, but you just said £25k, they may just go for the cheaper option.

During the interview you will get a good idea on if you feel you are gelling with the interviewer. Remember, you are interviewing them as much as they are interviewing you.

You need to decide if this is the type of company that you want to work for too. You will need to have a think about what is important for you at a company, this will help you with some questions you want to ask.

The Follow-Up

You're feeling confident after your interview. How do you now follow up? You need to send the hiring manager an email. At the end of the interview, all that remains is to wait: will you have given a good impression? For the position in question, will you or the intense competition be more suitable? How many other candidates have proposed themselves? How long will you still have to wait? Will you be given feedback in any case or will you no longer receive news?

It is practically impossible that you have not asked yourself at least one of these completely natural questions in your life. The possibility of being heard first - by preparing a follow-up email a few days after the interview - therefore becomes more and more inviting by the day.

Especially when you particularly like the job in question, this wait puts a strain on your nerves (and patience), even worse if recruiters wait a long time for hires or rejections. When you wait, time always seems to run slower. However, sending a follow-up email should definitely not be an impulsive initiative, without methodical reflection, after all, your professional future is at stake. We recommend that you read the following tips to contact the company and receive the answer you are waiting for without being intrusive.

If you were dealing with somebody else (perhaps someone in the admin team) to get your interview booked in, be sure to ask for the hiring manager's email address in your interview.

Wait a couple of hours before any correspondence. Firstly, find the interviewers on LinkedIn and add them with the following note;

'Hi [Name],

Was great to meet you today, thank you for taking the time to speak with me about the [job title] role.

[Your name]'

Short and sweet. Just to give them a reminder about you. They are also likely to have a little stalk of your LinkedIn profile, so make sure it's up to date and up to scratch.

The following morning you want to send your follow up email.

Good morning [name],

I hope you had a lovely rest of your day yesterday. It was really good to meet you, and I definitely feel I made the right decision in applying for the role at [company name].

I hope my experience working in the [relevant] industry and my [skill 1], [skill 2] and [skill 3] skills will show you I would make an excellent addition to your team. I felt we got on really well and I still need to hear about [something personal established in the interview. Did they have an upcoming trip? Did they tell you their pets name, a hobby they do?]

As promised please find attached [if you promised to send them anything during the interview]

Thank you again for taking the time to meet with me. If there is anything further I can do to support my application please let me know. Once again, it was great meeting you.

I look forward to hearing from you,
[Your name]
[Your mobile number]

They will normally reply and let you know when you can expect to hear from them. Most employers will be true to their word and let you know when they say they will, but things can come up out of their control so you may be waiting around. If they told you they were going to let you know by a certain date and they haven't, wait for three days before you chase. You never know what is going on (they could be ill, an emergency at work etc) and you don't want to add to any stress by messaging a day after they said they would.

In your follow up email you could say;
Hi [name],

Hope everything is all okay at your end. I just wanted to check in and see what the current situation is for the [job title] role?

Let me know if there is anything I can do to help the application process. I am free on [date 1], [date 2] and [date 3] to come back in if you're looking to do second interviews.

I look forward to hearing from you,
[Your name]

You should get a reply back from this, with an update on their hiring process. It will normally be met with an apology for taking so long! Depending on their response, it may also give you a clearer idea on whether the company is right for you.

Handling Rejections

You won't be offered every role. This doesn't mean you were not good enough, it just means they found someone else who they felt was better suited for the role, or they internally hired. You may never know.

Give yourself a pat on the back that you made it this far and you were considered for the role! The vital part now is to ensure you handle the rejection in the best manner possible. You don't want to close any doors with that company in the future. I once was told I wasn't going to be offered a role, because of how I went back to them they then asked me if I would be interested in another with them.

A step that everyone has to face is handling rejection. The job interview gone wrong is one of the steps that no one would want to experience. But that's part of the game, you can't start your job search without taking into account the possibility of being discarded. And to have done yet another interview to no avail. An interview that went wrong is, however, part of the wealth of knowledge and experience.

How can you tell if the interview went wrong? There can be many signs. The interviewer may hastily close the interview, or ignore the answers you give after they have asked you a question, perhaps from the point of view of posture and body language, they cross their arms and avoid eye contact with you. Could they be signs of failure? Yes. But don't anticipate that you have failed right away. There are a thousand ways to try to understand if a job interview went badly or well, in reality there could be just as many combinations to put you off track. During the interview, focus on the questions, then wait for the outcome. At the most, ask for clarity regarding the communication dates.

When they email you to let you know you were unsuccessful, it's common for it to be a copy and paste job and may not provide you with much information. You need feedback to help you when going to other interviews, and need to thank them for their time.

Hello [Name],

Thank you for your email. Whilst I am disappointed that I will not be your new [job title], I'm really pleased I made it this far in the process.

I'd love to get some feedback from you on why I was unsuccessful this time around? I'd really appreciate it as it would be really helpful for my self development and for potentially working with you again in the future.

It was lovely to meet with you, thank you for your time and if another role comes up that meets my skills and experience, please let me know.

Speak soon,
[Your name]

If you suspect that you were not taken forward in the application process or offered a job role because of your background, your first step should be to ask for feedback and clarification. It's clear that it is because of your ethnicity or culture, print out the proof, save it into a document. You should contact their HR team and Business Operations and explain. If they try to shush you and take it further - consider contacting citizens' advice.

We may have different religions, different languages, different coloured skin, but we all belong to one human race.

~ Kofi Annan

Difficult Conversations You May Have

There will be times when you need to have difficult conversations with your colleagues, or potentially your manager or senior leadership team. These may be conversations that eventually get escalated to the HR department or external HR companies. Some may be where you may have noticed something that somebody else said was inappropriate, someone may find something you said inappropriate, or it may be some unfair treatment or something that totally takes you by surprise.

The best thing you can do is be prepared on how to manage those conversations, and to understand what uncomfortable topics may come up.

If you know a difficult conversation is coming up, these are my top tips that you can follow to help yourself feel more comfortable and confident going into the situation.

- Reframe the conversation in your mind. If you're anticipating it's going to be a horrible conversation, you are going to dread it and feel anxious until it arrives. Frame it as an opportunity to discuss a grievance, and the outcome is going to be beneficial to all parties involved. Something will be learnt from the discussion, and policies may be changed. Go in with the mindset that you know who you are, and you I know you can make a difference.

- Understand why you are nervous. It's likely you may have been in this position before and it hasn't gone too well for you - which is understandable why you may feel this way. If you acknowledge how you are feeling, you're already taking a step in the right direction to try and alleviate those feelings.
- Get the meeting place right. You want your meeting to be in a mutually comfortable, secure and private space. Having this discussion for all of your colleagues to hear won't be beneficial to you or the other party. In someone's private office, boardroom or a corner in a coffee shop is the perfect setting for everybody to feel relaxed.
- Practice and prepare. Write out a list of items you want to address and discuss. Prepare questions that you want to ask and make notes on answers for questions you think you may be asked. You may not necessarily read straight from this document during, but having prepared yourself and having practised answering questions, will put you in good stead when you're in the meeting. It will help to keep you cool, calm and collected.
- Listen to the other party. Remember that as much as you want them to listen to you and to get your own point across, you need to listen to them too. You may feel they are wrong or offensive, but they may think this of you. You need to demonstrate the same level of listening and respect that you would expect.

- Give the other party time and space. You don't want them to feel attacked in this situation, give them time to articulate their thoughts and feelings and have a mature discussion.
- Prepare real evidence. Know this from when you first step foot into an office. Whenever something happens that you know isn't right - record it. Keep a log in your notes in your phone or in a notepad, so when it comes to these situations - you are able to back up what you are saying with facts.
- Bring a witness. You need to protect yourself. Ask a non biassed college to attend the meeting with you as a witness to the conversation. This person can ensure that everything being said and results are fair, and avoid any further grievances down the road.
- Create a plan for progress. Now the issue has been addressed, what is going to be put in place so this doesn't happen again going forward? Make sure in the meeting this is something that is addressed, as you don't want to feel like you are always in meetings talking about things that don't feel right.
- Finally, document the meeting. Ensure that during the meeting you are either taking notes or recording it. There needs to be a record of the meeting having taken place.

It's also worth doing some research on unions for your particular industry, and joining one to protect yourself.

Now, let's dive into some of those difficult conversations you could be having, or the comments that could spur on these difficult conversations.

Comments by other people you may have directed at you;
'I love your hair, can I touch it?'
'You're really [compliment] for someone who is [ethnic minority background]'
'I love chocolate men'
'So where are you really from?'
'How do [your race] feel about [any topic]'
'I haven't had an easy life so I don't have White Privilege'
'If I had to compare you to an animal, it would be a monkey'
'I think I have jungle fever'
'I'd love to set you up with someone. I think you'd like someone [same race as you]'
'Do you enjoy eating [food associated with your race as a stereotype]'
'[Any reference to slavery]'
'If I was [your race] for a day, I would [something inappropriate and stereotypical]'

There are hundreds of thousands of comments that could be made towards you, that will be inappropriate. These comments are specifically to do with race. ALL are wrong.

An important thing to remember, it is entirely up to you if you wish to educate somebody when they make an ignorant comment. You do not have to. It is not your job to teach others. It's your job to ensure you're making your environment as comfortable as you are able to. You must also remember that you are not a spokesperson for every person within your ethnicity. Just because I am a Mixed White British and Black Afro-Caribbean woman, does not mean I know the thoughts of everybody who shares my race.

That being said, should you choose to address the comments, you need to do it in the right way. The right way to ensure that if you do wish to take it further, you can.

There may also be scenarios where you feel a situation you are in is unjust, and the only reason is because of your ethnicity. For example, you may know for sure that you are the right person for a promotion or extra responsibilities. But somebody else is awarded the role.

The first thing you need to do is write down what has happened, and read it aloud to yourself. Does it still make sense? Explain the situation to friends/family, do they agree with you?

If yes, you need to address it with the person in which the incident occurred. The next time you see them, pull them to the side and ask if you can have a quick chat. Keeping it informal like this means they won't be on the defensive and you can explain to them how their comment made you feel, why you feel it was inappropriate and ask them to not do it again. If they are very nice about it, you can end the conversation on good terms. If they get defensive, make more rude comments or deny what they said, this is when you need to get HR or a senior member of staff involved.

At your next opportunity, speak to somebody else, explain the situation and how you tried to address it privately. This will then be escaped and the company will handle it in the appropriate manner. Follow the ten steps when they book in a meeting with you and the other party.

If the senior member of staff you have gone to isn't supportive, escalate the situation to someone who is even more senior than them. This may feel scary, but in order to make a positive impact you need to address these things.

Difficult conversations are hard. But by following these ten steps, and preparing yourself for how to address them, you're in the best position to address them, and create a better outcome.

Staying True to Yourself (Be Your Authentic Self)

Have you seen the movie 'Sorry to bother you'? It's based on a man called Cassius Green, who is a telemarketer and is struggling to make his way through the ranks. He's a Black man, and is constantly losing sales and getting hung up on. It's not until he adopts what is deemed as a 'White man's voice' that he becomes the coveted position of 'POWER CALLER'. This begs the question - can a Black person be their authentic self at work?

There is an argument that no person can be their true self at work. This is true to some extent, there is a level of professionalism that must be adhered to, as well as boundary setting. There is generally an expectation of keeping employees, namely White employees, comfortable at work. Sometimes you may find your White colleagues expecting you to adopt the role of the person who likes Hip-Hop music, who is good at dancing, who is 'different' and 'cool' and will tell them how every Black person sees the world. Not forgetting you may not even just be Black, you could be like be and be a mix of heritages. You may even find they wish to use you to explain away bad behaviour or to make themselves feel as if they are an ally. Have you ever heard the phrase 'It's fine I have Black friends'?

Professionalism is often seen as something that belongs to White people. This is evident from even a quick google search for hair styles as previously touched upon. Different hairstyles, languages and more are often regarded as unprofessional in the workplace. If you feel you are speaking in a certain way and can't have the hairstyle (that is part of your culture) you'd like to have at work, does this mean you are unable to turn up as your authentic self? And what ethnicity is this affecting more? The minority ethnicity.

In a system where it is hard for a person of colour to get their foot in the door, is it by any surprise that when they are, they feel the need to conform to 'Whiteness'. For ethnic minorities, it becomes the norm to change the way you talk, dress and act in order to meet a company's cultural fit. You may find that when you are entering a workplace, you feel as you walk into the building you are stripped of a lot of yourself. That you can't take your full self into the office.

But in the broader sense of things, don't we all play a role (sometimes)? Represent ourselves as stronger, more confident, or richer than we are? In fact, it's becoming increasingly rare to meet truly authentic people these days. In private life and especially at work. Because authenticity would mean standing up for weaknesses or allowing emotions. While some experts recommend playing a role at work and saving authenticity for private life, others see this as the key to success. Reason enough to take a closer look at the topic of "being authentic".

What do you personally understand by the term "authenticity"? Most people would probably call it "just be yourself". And that's not all that wrong: Experts see authenticity as the ability to present oneself and act in a way that corresponds to one's own nature. Authentic people are therefore free from falsifications, external influences or playing a role. But this also goes hand in hand with standing by your weaknesses, being able to show your emotions and therefore also being vulnerable. And despite the fact that authenticity makes us more vulnerable than playing the unflinching, tough, and unfeeling person, we're happier as authentic people. How so? Because authenticity leads to an inner freedom, it dissolves self-doubt, inner constraints and complexes.

It might feel difficult at first to be your authentic self. I've never liked the moments I've walked into the office with a new hairstyle, or spoken about something I did on the weekend and it wasn't seen as the norm. It was normal to ME. But I carried on. I carried on going in with my hairstyles and loud outfits. Because I knew the more I exposed people to it (hopefully), the more likely they were to accept these things as normal.

You have to do what you feel comfortable doing. I will never make you feel bad for hiding certain elements of yourself if you feel it is going to help you. I just want to remind you of the importance it is to show up as your true self.

You're making it easier for the generation after you. The more people who can be their true selves now, the more people who will be able to be their true selves in the years to come.
You're exposing people to and educating them about different cultures. When somebody has seen your latest hairstyle, you can open them up to a conversation about it. And in turn open this up to a conversation about different cultures.

You're protecting your culture. By owning who you are, and showing you will not hide it or conform to any structural racism or questionable standards, you are saying YES this is who I am and I am PROUD. You're making it easier for other colleagues to do the same, who may not have felt confident if you hadn't made that step. You're making it easier for yourself. You can be yourself. Every day. You don't need to put up any walls and become something that you are not.

Yes, it won't feel easy at first. But I promise you that you will get there. Maybe not at the first place you work, or even the second, but the energy you put out into the universe will come back for you. If you consistently show up as your authentic self, be proud of who you are, you will eventually find a place of work where you feel home.

Those who manage to live authentically gain new self-confidence over the long term, the courage for even more authenticity and thus a high degree of credibility in their appearance. And this is known to be an important success factor for employees, managers and politicians.

So is authenticity the key to success?

Does authenticity automatically make you happy?

Unfortunately, it's not quite that simple. While authenticity is certainly a good goal for everyone, that doesn't mean that you should act out your quirks, tantrums, or crying fits at all times and completely uninhibitedly. Sure, emotions and weaknesses are absolutely human and it is well known that nobody is perfect. And yet, despite living authenticity, we should never stop working on ourselves. There is a difference between the so-called reflected and the unreflected authenticity: The unreflected authenticity can quickly shoot you out, especially professionally. It is therefore important that you know yourself, your behaviour, character traits, strengths and weaknesses as well as wishes and needs and reflect on them at regular intervals.

How quickly do you get angry?
How do you deal with conflicts?
What makes you happy?
Where are your strengths?
What weaknesses should you work on?

However, only a few people dare to reflect ruthlessly and honestly on themselves. That in turn means admitting weaknesses and mistakes, and that hurts. But that is also part of being authentic.

Being authentic at work – is that even possible?

In surveys, many executives, especially the female ones, state that they want to appear authentic. Critics, on the other hand, see authenticity in professional life as completely out of place. After all, employees in managerial positions have a leadership role. And the word speaks for itself. Take a look around your company: Do you find the managers to be authentic? And is it you?

Authenticity at work is important. Take Viola Davis, one of the best actresses there has ever been. She is honest about how hard she has worked, as well as how much harder it is for her as a Black woman, and shares those hardships along with her successes. People who authentically stand by their opinions and beliefs and align their actions and goals with them can inspire and motivate other people, or are simply very respected.

Can you also be "Too Authentic"? Too authentic? Doesn't that actually contradict itself? No, because this is exactly where we have to draw the line between private and professional life. There may not be too much authenticity in private life, but there is in professional life. Especially when you are in a management position, there is also a limit above which authenticity is out of place. This is in your private life: Your marital problems, the desire to have children or other excessive openness regarding your private life circumstances do not belong in the job. Although this information makes you more accessible as a person and perhaps also more human as a manager in the eyes of your employees, unfortunately this type of authenticity in professional life is still all too often seen as a weakness and mercilessly exploited. You should therefore find a new kind of authenticity in your job: a professional authenticity, so to speak, that corresponds to your personality and your convictions, but at the same time does not reveal too much about your private life.

It is important that you learn when to differentiate between professional and private authenticity. So what does "professional authenticity" mean?

Anyone who has the feeling that they have to play a role every day in their job in order to be recognized or to advance professionally will usually not be happy in the long run. Having to play a role five, six or seven days a week, for eight, nine or even ten hours a day: that is incredibly exhausting and therefore often ends in burnout sooner or later.

So start by being authentic at work. According to the expert opinion of business coach Simone von Stosch, such "professional" authenticity includes the following aspects:
A healthy self-esteem is the cornerstone of authenticity, but is also strengthened by it at the same time. So get

into the positive upward spiral of self-confidence and being authentic.
Self-reflection should accompany you throughout your life, both privately and professionally. But this also includes the courage to admit painful insights and to make changes in one's own life or in one's own person.

Values and beliefs are the cornerstone of your authentic actions. What do you stand for as a person? Where are your limits? Stand up for it and you will automatically earn the respect of your employees. Of course, goals, beliefs, or even values can evolve or change throughout life. But not overnight. Therefore, even when you encounter obstacles, remain yourself. That way, your employees will know when to count on you, when to get angry, when to be happy, etc. Nothing worse than a boss who responds to the same problem with a smile one day and cholerically the next. Because that is an unmistakable sign of either unreflected authenticity or a played role from which the person repeatedly breaks out unintentionally.

It is usually not possible to play a role permanently. Ultimately, we are all just human beings with emotions, fears, weaknesses and needs. And at the latest in really stressful or stressful situations, many people show their true colours. So don't play a role anymore, instead opt for authenticity. Learn to distinguish between professional and private authenticity. Do you have the feeling that you cannot live authentically in your job or your environment? Or if you are authentic, do you suddenly have doubts about your choice of profession or company? Then now is the time to act. You will see that living authentically is happier, more relaxed and, with the art of reflected authenticity, also more successful.

Finance Template

For some reason (structural racism), it's harder for an ethnic minority to save money, buy a house, make investments and more. I was very fortunate that I bought my first property when I was 23 years old. I had some help from my mum and saved myself for the deposit and all of the solicitor's fees. But to be able to borrow the rest from the bank, and to have had the skills to save was all from myself.

In my first Marketing job, I had possibly the best boss ever. She was so supportive and was always pushing me to better myself and go further. I looked at her and saw the success that I too wanted to achieve. This is where I developed my drive. I started saving in that first 'career' job. (Prior to this I worked part time at Argos and was very much living a 'work hard, party hard' lifestyle!)

Because the odds are naturally stacked against minority ethnicities, you need to work harder in order to achieve the same thing. You still need to live your life and get enjoyment out of it, create experiences and pay for your bills, BUT you need to save too. Call it a rainy day fund, a new car or a deposit for your first property, you need something to fall back on. It's recommended that you have at least 3 months worth of your wages saved in your bank account at any one time.

Let's work with the example that your first full time entry level role comes with a salary of £20,000. This means after tax, you will take home £1437 every month. The general rule is 50% of your wage is for needs, 30% for wants and 20% for savings. 50% of your monthly wage is £718. £431 equates to 30%, so the total for needs and wants is £1149, meaning you need to save a minimum of £288 a month.

Rent/Bills - £800
Food shop - £120
Phone - £50
Gym - £50
Music/film subscriptions - £20
Monthly bus pass - £40
Misc (friends birthdays, food out etc) - £69

Being overly generous with your budgeting (you could find a gym cheaper than £50 a month, or your food shop may be less) you're much more likely to consistently save a good amount. £288 a month for a year is £3456.

Now imagine that the following year you get a salary increase. Your savings will go up. If you start this consistently from a young age, you will have a nice saving pot quicker than you know it.

£20,000 a year with 20% in savings = £3456
£22,000 a year with 20% in savings = £3720
£24,000 a year with 20% in savings = £3996
£26,000 a year with 20% in savings = £4272
£28,000 a year with 20% in savings = £4336
£30,000 a year with 20% in savings = £4800

Based on the example your first 'career' job starts at the age of 17, and you consistently work hard and get a promotion with a raise consistently, by the time you are 25, you could have around £25,000 saved up.

With this you could invest in property, start your own business, go travelling, or even just carry on saving until you know what you want to do with it!

There will be times when you won't want to save the money, or you want to dip into those savings. This is why you need to ensure the amount you are saving each month is reasonable enough that you are still enjoying your life. Following this template will give you the best chance of not falling into the statistic of ethnic minorities having a harder time financially.

Managing finances according to a Harvard economist, comes down to 10 essential rules. Money doesn't grow on trees, so not only do you have to work for it, but you also have to be smart with your earnings by saving and investing. First of all, you often make losses without realising it (e.g. you get loose change in coins and you drop a few or they get lost under the couch), and according to the experts, opening a savings account is not always enough to have.

The elite Harvard University has published several articles dealing with financial management, including one by economist Laurence J. Kotlikoff; it describes rules and recommendations that are helpful in managing money as sustainably as possible.

1. Live future-oriented
This applies to both your private life and your career. According to Kotlikoff, it's important to consider whether the job you have now is right for you, whether the position you are in may be at risk, and whether you are taking the necessary precautions to be able to live in old age as you imagine. You may feel like your 65th birthday is still a long way off, but it's important to start turning the right gears from an early age.

2. You need a budget
A budget is very useful when you want to manage your finances. It gives you an overview of how high your expenses are, what you can save and how much of your salary you can save without having to make radical sacrifices. Setting a budget will even help you identify the small (potentially unnecessary) expenses that will have a big impact on your finances in the long run.

3. Avoid too many credit cards
It's true that you need a credit card for certain things, but you shouldn't have too many of them. Remember that you have to pay for everything you buy, and having more cards to pay off that debt will only leave you with more debt that will become increasingly difficult to pay off over time.

4. Save consistently

It's not about saving hundreds of dollars every month . It's important that you start putting money into your savings account, even if it's just a small amount. Experts also recommend that you think about investing because it not only saves your money but also helps you grow it month after month, but for that you may need the help of an advisor to guide you.

5. Set goals

Having goals is the starting point for creating a budget, for knowing if you need to be a little more economical with your spending, or for motivating and psychologically preparing yourself to spend a certain amount every time you get your money to put aside.

6. Don't retire early

Retirement, according to Kotlikoff, is actually the longest and most expensive vacation of your life. So unless you're a multi-millionaire, be aware that if you retire early, you may not have enough money or be unable to maintain the lifestyle you want long enough.

7. Keep moving professionally

Dare to take calculated risks, look for better opportunities, analyse better offers—even use it as an opportunity to demand a raise or a job promotion.

8. Buy instead of rent

Yes, it's tough and maybe expensive, but rent has a major impact on your finances, especially as rents can increase over time and due to inflation. It is advisable that you decide to buy, bearing in mind that there are properties that are like an investment as they can appreciate in value and you can get a good deal on sale.

9. As you spend, ask yourself these questions
Before you buy anything, especially if it is an expensive purchase, you should ask yourself some important questions:
Do I really need this?
Do I have to have it immediately?
What if I don't buy it right away?
How have I been able to survive without this purchase?

10. Ask yourself these questions before taking out a loan
Loans can be very useful in such a case, but if you don't take care of yourself, you can lose a lot of money. Ask yourself about it:
Character: How well are you able to meet your financial obligations?
Capacity: How easy will it be for you to pay off your debt?
Collateral: If you have very large loans or expenses, what will secure them?

By following these tips and setting your own goals and budgets, you'll be able to take charge of your finances, and set yourself up for success.

Benefits of Gratitude, Planning and Journaling

I'm sure you've heard/read it in many places, coming from a sceptic, these things work. Let's start off with planning. Planning is a huge stress-management tool. Picture this, you've just spent two weeks on holiday and are coming back to work during a busy period for the office on a Monday. Your inbox is full to the brim, everybody is in meetings and you have nobody to lean on. What can you do?

First, however, typical objections to planning should be mentioned and then refuted. The following two arguments are frequently used against planning: Planning is too time consuming and limits spontaneity.

Overall, planning is pointless because plans that have been drawn up cannot be implemented because the future is unpredictable. However, these objections are immediately resolved if the following considerations are taken into account: Planning deals with the part of the tasks that are predictable. By carrying out this work in a planned manner, there is more time for unforeseen and spontaneous activities. The aim of proper planning is not to take on and complete more tasks. Planning must never become an end in itself. Carefully prepared plans are important, but implementation remains crucial.

Benefits of planning
- You develop clear ideas about your projects and tasks

- You can stay focused on your goals and better manage distractions
- By being mentally prepared, you can use your time more effectively
- When planning, new ideas for better execution of tasks often come up
- You relieve your memory

Get your notebook out, and your calendar and plan your day. Create a to do list and categorise by priorities and deadlines. Once you've done this you can allocate your tasks to your diary and understand when you're going to start/finish these things. I stand by my notebooks and Google calendar for organising my whole life. Acting on your to-do list, instead of reacting when you panic as things mount up, is proven to reduce stress and will lead to more fulfilling living. It will also help you to learn more and retain that information. Writing out your plans by hand and things you need to accomplish is beneficial to your brain and your goals will stay 'stuck' in your head.

It will also help you keep track of both long and short term goals. Putting pen to paper and seeing them will help you to visualise and actualise your goals. If you spend at least 10-20 minutes per day, this will naturally make you more present in the moment and make you more intentional and mindful.

Being mindful will increase your fulfilment. Being grateful will increase your fulfilment. How can you express your gratitude? Journaling.

I'm not asking you to write a full page every day. You don't even need to write this on paper, even keeping a pinned note in your Notes app will be helpful. At the end of the day, just choose one thing that you are grateful for. Sometimes you may write a few paragraphs, sometimes it may be one word. But do it. In a month you will notice a huge difference to the fulfilment you have in your life.

Set priorities!
If you have completed the last chapter, you have developed a clear idea of your goals. Next, it's important to prioritise these goals—think of which task is important to the achievement of your goals. That is why criteria for setting priorities now follow.

First, ask yourself: Does the task you are about to perform have long-term significance? Or is it something urgent at short notice? Both types of tasks play an important role in our lives. By setting your priorities correctly, you will ensure that you get the tasks that are urgent in the short term as well as the tasks that are important in the long term. One of the main causes of stress is not getting important things done, which you can avoid by doing this.

A priorities
We designate tasks that bring the greatest benefit and important results for the achievement of your long-term

goals as A-priorities. Examples would be working on a report or renovating a living space.

B priorities
B priorities are regularly recurring tasks that arise in the household (shopping, cleaning, etc.) and work (correspondence, bookkeeping, filing, etc.). They form the basis of your A-priorities and can often be delegated, but must not be neglected.

C Priorities
C priorities are activities that are not relevant to your long-term goals or recurring tasks. You tend to spend most of your time on B priorities. However, you should use your best time, i.e. the time of your personal peak performance, for the A priorities. Plan at least one priority per day and complete this task as early as possible. The important things first! If you follow this principle, you will experience a sense of achievement every day: you have come one step closer to your goals.

Setting priorities is one thing, sticking to them is another. We are constantly faced with interruptions from visitors, phone calls, colleagues, etc. In order to comply with priorities, it is important to only allow disruptions at certain, specified times in justified exceptional cases. Constant interruptions are a distraction and often the important task remains unfinished. Concentrate on what is important to you and ignore the irrelevant.

Quiet hour
Schedule a "quiet hour" at the beginning of your workday. Check with co-workers or family members and set aside an hour (or more) a day when you won't disturb each other. Make yourself unavailable for this period, ie don't answer the phone or answer the doorbell when it rings. An hour a day when you can work on your most important task without disruption has a huge impact on your effectiveness. Therefore, only allow yourself to be prevented from doing so in emergencies and for appointments that cannot be postponed.

Plan in projects
The aim of planning is not to do everything , but to do the most important things . Project planning allows you to focus on the important and long-term projects amidst thousands of things that want to take up your time. It prevents you from getting bogged down. Therefore, when planning, think in terms of projects. A project is any task or activity that consists of three or more steps. A project can be as big as starting your own business, or as small as renovating a home.

You can plan projects in the following ways:
Description of the desired goal. When renovating a living space, the goal could be to create a cosy space by applying a new coat of paint and laying a carpet.
Structure of the project in subtasks. When renovating, for example, the following subtasks arise: buying paint and other materials, clearing the furniture out of the room, painting, laying the carpet. Play through the

process of your project in your mind. A sketch of the necessary steps can help ensure that important subtasks are not forgotten. Also check whether you have all the skills required to carry it out or whether you need to acquire specialist knowledge beforehand or perhaps want to delegate subtasks.

Determination of the required means and resources. Assign the resources you need to complete each subtask. Then it cannot happen that you want to start painting the door and suddenly find that there is no adhesive tape to mask the door frame.Setting the start and end dates and estimating the time required. Plan backwards. In the renovation example, this means: First, the dates for painting and laying the carpet are planned. After that, dates for purchasing the material etc. can be set. Be realistic about the time it takes you to complete each task. Transfer the specified tasks and deadlines from your project plan to your respective daily or weekly plan.

With the help of project planning, a task that you feel overwhelmed by can be broken down into manageable steps and often lose its terror as a result.

Make appointments!
We often only think negatively about deadlines that are set for us to complete a task. We feel under pressure and complain about the stress that an approaching appointment triggers in us. And probably everyone feels bad when they can't keep an appointment.

However, deadlines can also be viewed positively. We can change our mindset and see setting appointments as a good way to manage our own time and relieve unnecessary stress. Setting deadlines is about not wanting tasks to take up more time than necessary. So set yourself realistic dates. Measure the progress of your work against your time constraints and refuse interruptions for less important reasons.Meeting the deadlines you set yourself gives you a deeply satisfying sense of accomplishment. They are happy about the proven self-discipline and motivate themselves for the next task or can really enjoy a break.

Plan for results!
How do you plan your appointments? Do you make a note in your schedule book like "3 p.m. meeting with colleague Meier" and then wait for the appointment? Or are you actively preparing for an appointment? Be clear about what this meeting is about, what outcomes you are aiming for. So don't just set aside the time you need, but think about what you want to discuss, plan, or accomplish during that appointment.

Important: Don't just reserve time, but determine the results you want to achieve. Record these desired outcomes in detail in your schedule book. For example, instead of writing "9:00 am - Report" write "9:00 am - Drafting an outline for a project report. Write a first draft".

The most important part of planning is regular written planning for the next day. Knowing exactly what you want to get done in a day is the only way to avoid interruptions and distractions. If you don't have a precise idea of the tasks you want to do, there is a risk that other people and not you yourself will determine your working day.

Example:
Claudia is an accountant. On Monday she starts work at 7.30 am sharp because she wants to finish the monthly accounts. In the office, she meets a colleague from the purchasing department and talks to him for ten minutes. After that, she opens her mail and takes care of the correspondence. She is repeatedly interrupted at work by inquiries from colleagues and phone calls. From 10.30 a.m. she works again with interruptions of about 90 minutes on the monthly closing. After the lunch break, she has to go to a meeting that lasts longer than expected. After all, Claudia has to work overtime in order to be able to complete the monthly statement as planned.

Claudia could have organised this working day better. Since closing the month-end was by far her most important task that day, she should have started it immediately at 7:30 am. She could have asked her colleagues not to interrupt her with inquiries until 10:30 am and a secretary would have answered all calls for her until then. She would have finished the monthly statement by 10:30 a.m. and left on time in the evening without having to work overtime. She could have done her mail and phone calls between 10:30 a.m. and lunchtime.

The work result of both daily routines is the same. In the second case, however, Claudia saves herself overtime through better planning and can enjoy her free time instead.

What does a promising day plan look like for you? At the end of your working day, get in the habit of planning the coming day in writing. Determine the task(s) that you definitely want to accomplish (i.e. your A-priority(s)). Be realistic about how much time this will take you. Then set your B priorities. Plan only about 50 to 60% of your working time in total, so that you have enough time for the unforeseen.

The daily routine
When planning your day, also consider a daily routine that reduces stress as much as possible and lets you complete your tasks with inner peace. Please note the following points in particular.

The beginning of the day
Start the day calmly. It's better to get up a little earlier so that you don't have to leave the house under time pressure without having breakfast. Take the time for a pleasant start to the day and thereby create the conditions for optimal performance and inner balance.

Your performance
What times of the day are you most productive? For many people, this is the early morning hours. Check whether this also applies to you and then use these times for your most important tasks.

Breaks
Studies show that breaks are necessary to stay productive. The recovery is greatest in the first three minutes of a break. Several short breaks in addition to the longer lunch break help you to stay productive. Use these breaks primarily to get up and move around.

Balance
Pay attention to "balanced" daily planning. Therefore, do not just take on similar activities that then seem tiring. Make a change. Don't just think about your professional activities, but plan time for sports and friends.

The weekly plan
On Friday of the previous week you can set the goals for the following week. For the weekly planning, you need an overview of the times that are already scheduled for appointments, short trips, etc. Weekly plans have the advantage that you can move the planned activities back and forth to suit. Think about the day on which you can probably reach individual destinations most cheaply. Every day can be used better because you have the opportunity to combine tasks in a meaningful way.

You can take goals for the week from your project plans or you can include tasks that arise at short notice.

Again, plan not only your professional but also your private projects. Make the most of the evenings and weekends with lots of interesting activities.

The monthly plan
In one month you can achieve a lot for your long-term goals. You compile your monthly goals in writing from your annual goals, your project plans, uncompleted tasks, new plans and unforeseen events. The weekly and daily goals are then derived from this.

Set a focus for each month.
These priorities can also be influenced by the season, such as "go skiing regularly on the weekends in February", or be derived from your annual goals, such as "try a new dish three times a week in the evening", if you set yourself the goal to learn to cook.

The annual plan
A year is a period that is not easy to survey and which therefore often causes difficulties in planning. However, there are often time periods in which many activities are already known that can be taken into account in the planning. So maybe the time and duration of the vacation is already fixed. Or there are already fixed exam dates, the preparation of which can be planned. Larger family celebrations or a move are other examples of already established events.

Sometimes it makes life difficult to focus on the positive aspects of life. When it comes to your diet, you might notice the days when you ate too much or missed your sports session.

Success experiences are not valued appropriately and failures come to the fore. Negative thoughts lead to stress, which in turn leads to further failures. The feeling quickly arises that everything is going badly, which can lead to a downward spiral.

You can prevent such downward spirals by consciously concentrating on the small successes in your life. Gratitude is good for your psyche and your body, which leads to more success and joy in your life.

Benefit 1: Gratitude strengthens your heart
Negative thoughts lead to the release of stress hormones. These put a strain on your psyche in the long run and worsen your mood even further. But your body also suffers from them. The heart is often particularly stressed. People who suffer from a lot of stress can develop serious problems such as heart failure or high blood pressure. The susceptibility to heart attacks can also increase.

So focusing too much on the negative in your life can lead to serious health problems that can even become life-threatening. It is therefore highly recommended that you consciously focus on the positive. The beneficial effects of positive thoughts on the heart have been scientifically proven. According to one study 1 , by adopting a conscious attitude of gratitude, subjects could increase their heart rate variability and reduce the risk of a heart attack. Their susceptibility to inflammation also decreased. So practise being thankful for the little things in life and strengthen your heart. Negative thoughts burden your heart. Heart problems can be distressing or even hazardous to health. A grateful attitude to life can reduce heart problems.

Benefit 2: Gratitude reduces insomnia
Constantly circling around negative thoughts can lead to massive sleep disorders . You too have certainly had sleepless nights in which you couldn't get out of your brooding. Problems and failures often seem bigger the longer you think about them. There are also fewer distractions at night than during the day. This makes it even easier to focus on the negative.

Insomnia is a natural response to stress because stress hormones put the body on high alert. In order to be able to fall asleep better again , you should pay attention to your thoughts and try to consciously influence them positively. Improving sleep through positive thinking was studied by world-renowned gratitude researcher Alex M. Woods. In their studies, Woods and his team were able to prove 2 that grateful people sleep better and more deeply. Thanks to better and more restful sleep, the subjects were also more productive overall.

So if you suffer from insomnia, it may well be that these have to do with negative thoughts. Try to also focus on the positive things in your life and also appreciate small successes. Better sleep will not only make you more productive, but also more balanced and happier. Negative thoughts can cause insomnia. Gratitude can improve your sleep. The better you sleep, the happier and more productive you are.

Benefit 3: Gratitude reduces stress
When negative thoughts are part of everyday life, your body finds it difficult to relax. The flooding of your body with stress hormones can become chronic and lead to mental illnesses such as depression or anxiety disorders. Gratitude has been shown to make a difference in your stress levels. This was shown by studies by Martin Seligman and Tracy Stephen 3 at the University of Pennsylvania. With conscious positive thinking, the study participants were able to lower their own stress level and break through negative thought patterns. As a result, they were not only more resistant to stress in everyday life - their susceptibility to mental illness was also reduced.

Negative thoughts lead to stress.
Persistent stress can result in mental illness.Gratitude can break through negative thought patterns. Be happier with a gratitude journal. Positive thinking is difficult for many people. However, that doesn't mean it can't be learned. If you also notice that you keep falling into negative feelings, don't appreciate successes

appropriately and only concentrate on failures and disappointments, then realise what you can be thankful for in your life. With conscious gratitude, you can relearn positive thinking. To integrate positive thinking into your everyday life, a gratitude journal can be very helpful. Every night think of three things you are grateful for and write them down in your journal. These can be situations, people, feelings, a sense of achievement or even objects.

It is important that the entries relate to the day in question and that you always find something new to be grateful for. The entries should also concern you personally and not be formulated too generally. This exercise can help you to see and appreciate even the small things in your everyday life. The more you focus on the positive things in your life, the happier you will be.

Glossary of Terms

Whilst there are so many words that will come under the umbrella of 'words you should know' in regards to structural racism, discrimination etc., these are the ones I have (deemed myself) very important that you should not only know the word, but understand the meaning too.

Ally ship
The practice of emphasising social justice, inclusion, and human rights by members of an ingroup, to advance the interests of an oppressed or marginalised outgroup. A lifelong process of building relationships based on trust, consistency, and accountability with marginalised individuals and/or groups of people.

Anti-racist
A form of action against racism and the systemic racism and the oppression of marginalised groups. Being antiracist is based on the conscious efforts and actions to provide equitable opportunities for all people on an individual and systemic level.

BIPOC
Acronym that stands for Black. Indigenous. People of Colour. A more inclusive term than "people of colour" when talking about marginalised groups affected by racism.

Critical Race Theory
Critical Race Theory is a school of thought that says that legal institutions and the law are inherently racist. A theoretical framework in the social sciences that examines society and culture as they relate to categorizations of race, law, and power. It is loosely unified by two common themes.

Cultural Appropriation
The adoption of an element of one culture or identity by members of another culture or identity. This can be controversial when members of a dominant culture appropriate from disadvantaged minority cultures.

Diversity, Equity and Inclusion (DEI)
Used in corporate spaces to encompass efforts by business leaders to make their spaces more diverse, fair, and inclusive. Diversity is often perceived to be about perspective, representation, tough conversation, and supporting inclusion. Inclusion prompts answers about creating environments conducive to feedback, supporting diversity, and being open. Equity was described as fairness, sameness, and valuing diversity and inclusion.

Microaggression
Indirect expressions of racism, sexism, ageism, ableism, or another form of prejudice. They can be in seemingly harmless comments from people who might be well-intentioned. But they make another person feel different, violated, or unsafe.

Reparations
Refers to payment for harm or damage. It mainly refers to payments for harm and damage done to Black Americans who have endured decades of slavery, Jim Crow laws, racial violence, racist education and housing laws, and prejudice.

Unconscious Bias
There is explicit bias, or bias we're aware of, and then there's implicit bias, or prejudicial beliefs we don't even know we have. Unconscious biases are social stereotypes about certain groups of people that individuals form outside their own conscious awareness. Unconscious bias is far more prevalent than conscious prejudice and often incompatible with one's conscious values.

White Fragility
A state in which even a minimum amount of racial stress becomes intolerable, triggering a range of defensive moves," including "the outward display of emotions such as anger, fear, and guilt, and behaviours such as argumentation, silence, and leaving the stress-inducing situation.

White Privilege
The vast set of advantages and benefits that people have solely because they are white or pass as white. Generally white people who experience such privilege do so without being conscious of it. Examples include

being able to walk around in a department store without being followed by a retail assistant who suspects you of shoplifting or being able to drive around a town without fearing that someone will call the police on you.

Books you should read
Knowledge = power. I never recommend a book that I haven't read myself, and I never recommend a book for the sake of it.

This list of books genuinely helped me in one way or another, whether that was my self confidence, helping create a better circle around me, planning my days and time better etc etc.

Whilst I may not agree with everything written in each of these books, it's still great to read other people's perspectives whether you believe in the same or not. It still educates you.

Without further ado and in no particular order..

Good Vibes, Good Life by Vex King
Healing is the new high by Vex King
Heart and Hustle - Patricia Bright
The Pursuit of Happyness - Chris Gardner
Little Black Book by Otegha Uwagba
Happy Sexy Millionaire by Steven Bartlett

101 Black Owned Businesses you can shop from

I've curated a list of Black owned businesses here that you can shop from!

Many of them are very small, some are large businesses but they are all independently owned by an ethnic minority that you can support!

Afro Drops
https://afrodrops.com/

Afrocenchix
https://afrocenchix.com/

Alero Jasmine
https://www.alerojasmine.com/

Almocado
https://www.almocado.com/

Antidote Street
https://antidotestreet.com/

Ashanti Swimwear
https://www.ashantiswimwear.com/

Avila Diana
https://aviladiana.com/

Aysha Bell Wellness

https://www.ayshabell.com/home

BadGal Online
https://www.badgalonline.com/

Bea Skincare
https://www.bea-skincare.com/

Bespoke Binny
https://bespokebinny.com/

Bokitla
https://www.bokitla.com/

Boucleme
https://www.boucleme.co.uk/

Bourn Beautiful
https://www.bournbeautifulnaturals.uk/

By Aaron Wallace
https://byaaronwallace.com/

Caribbean Magic
https://www.caribbeanmagics.com/

Casely-Hayford
https://casely-hayford.com/

Charlotte Mensah
https://www.charlottemensah.com/

Chilli Chop Co
https://www.etsy.com/uk/shop/ChilliChopCo

Chloe Ainsley Creative
https://www.chloeainsleycreative.co.uk/

Colour Celebrations
https://colourcelebrations.com/

Copper Dust
https://www.copperdustlondon.com/

Cultureville
https://www.cultureville.co.uk/

Damihow
https://www.damihow.com/

Dar-Leone
https://www.dar-leone.com/

Dark Sugars
https://www.darksugars.co.uk/

Darren Scott Salon
https://www.darrenscottsalon.com/

Deserted Cactus
https://www.instagram.com/deserted_cactus/

Detola and Geek
https://www.detolaandgeek.com/

Dizziak
https://dizziak.com/

Dorcas Creates
https://dorcascreates.com/

Duodu London
https://duodulondon.co.uk/

Dvees
https://www.dvees.com/

Eat of Eden
https://eatofeden.co.uk/

Elsie and Fred
https://www.elsieandfred.com/

Equi Botanics
https://www.equibotanics.com/

Everyday Froday
https://everydayfroday.com/

Fish, Wings & Tings
https://fishwingsandtings.com/home/

Freya Bramble Carter

https://freyabramblecarter.com/

Fundi Box
https://www.fundibox.co.uk/

Goch and Co
https://www.gochandcompany.co/home

Goodman Factory
https://www.goodmanfactory.com/

HEZA
https://www.heza.co.uk/

House of Keems
https://houseofkeems.com/

Imagine Me Stories
https://www.imaginemestories.com/

Kalabash
https://www.kalabashbodycare.com/

Kaz Vare Made It
https://kazvaremadeit.com/

Kemi Telford
https://kemitelford.com/

Kitsch Noir
https://kitschnoir.com/

Knots
http://knots-uk.com/

Kosibah
https://kosibah.com/

Labrum
https://labrumlondon.com/

Las Olas
https://www.lasolasrumclub.com/

Liha Beauty
https://lihabeauty.com/

Luxe More London
https://www.luxemorelondon.com/

Make-Up Addiction
https://www.makeupaddictioncosmetics.com/

Mamater
https://www.mamater.com/

Manicure You
https://www.manicureyou.com/

Marcia Vidal
https://www.marciavidal.co.uk/

Martine Rose
https://martine-rose.com/

Matugga Rum
https://www.matuggarum.com/

Maya Nije
http://www.mayanjie.com/

MDM Flow
https://mdmflow.com/

Mom Made UK
https://www.etsy.com/uk/shop/MommadeUK

Mr Blackman's
https://www.mrblackmans.com/

Muffin Sisters
https://www.muffinsisters.com/

Naked Clay Ceramics
https://www.nakedclayceramics.com/

New Beacon Books   Book Publisher
https://www.newbeaconbooks.com

Nicola Lespeare
https://www.nicolalespeare.com/

Nubian Skin
https://www.nubianskin.com/

Oil of Nature
https://www.oilofnature.co.uk/

Our Kids Trove
https://ourkidstrove.com/

Our Lovely Goods
https://ourlovelygoods.com/

Pamoja
https://pamojaskincare.com/

Pelicans and Parrots
http://pelicansandparrots.com/

Philly and Friends
https://phillyandfriends.com/

Pigment Perfect
https://www.pigmentperfect.co.uk/

Plum & Rabbits
https://plumbandrabbitts.co.uk/

Prick
https://www.prickldn.com/

Renee's Kitchen
https://www.instagram.com/renees.kitchen/

Rita Colson
https://www.ritacolson.com/

Sancho's Home
https://sanchosshop.com/

Selfmade Candle
https://selfmadecandle.com/

Sheni and Teni
https://sheniandteni.com/

Skimdo
https://www.skimdo.com/

Soapsmith
https://soapsmith.com/

The Afro Hair and Skin Company
https://www.theafrohairandskincompany.co.uk/

The Chalk House
https://www.thechalkhouse.com/

The Undergarment
https://theunderargument.com/

Thes Lac Rose
https://en.theslacrose.com/

Thimble and Doll
https://www.thimbleanddoll.co.uk/

Three Little Birds
https://www.threelittlebirdsja.com/

Tihara Smith
https://www.tiharasmith.com/

Tribal Unicorn
https://www.tribal-unicorn.com/

Uncle John's Bakery
https://theunclejohnsbakery.com/

Uptown Yardie
https://uptownyardie.com/

VSmine
https://www.vsmine.co.uk/

Wales Bonner
https://walesbonner.net/

We are Lagom
https://www.wearelagom.com/

Yako Beauty
https://www.yakobeauty.com/

Zoe's Ghana Kitchen
https://www.zoesghanakitchen.com/

So I suppose that brings this book to an end. I hope you've found it insightful, and will help you in some way.

Please reach out to me on Instagram (@bymeganwellman) or LinkedIn (/in/meganwellman), or you can join my slack community (also called Flourish) which you can find via my LinkedIn profile.

I'd love to hear your thoughts on this book, and if there is anything you feel I could help you with, or if there is anything else you'd like to see from me!

Thank you from the bottom of my heart for supporting me and investing in this book.

Megan x

References

https://www.brookings.edu/research/following-the-success-sequence-success-is-more-likely-if-youre-white/

https://www.dailymail.co.uk/femail/article-3527717/Student-left-shocked-Google-search-unprofessional-hairstyles-work-features-black-women.html

https://medium.com/the-post-grad-survival-guide/headhunter-presents-how-to-go-the-extra-mile-at-an-interview-7a69751ad613

https://resumegenius.com/faq/how-many-skills-should-you-list-on-a-resume

https://www.icslearn.co.uk/blog/posts/2020/november/12-tips-for-handling-difficult-conversations-at-work/

Neville, H. A., Worthington, R. L., & Spanierman, L. B. (2001). Race, power, and multicultural counseling psychology: Understanding white privilege and colour-blind racial attitudes. In J. G. Ponterotto, J. M. Casas, L. A. Suzuki, & C. M. Alexander (Eds.), Handbook of multicultural counseling (pp. 257–288). Sage Publications, Inc.

https://www.nasponline.org/resources-and-publications/resources-and-podcasts/diversity-and-social-justice/social-justice/sp4sj-podcast-and-google-hangout-series/understanding-white-privilege

https://deepblue.lib.umich.edu/handle/2027.42/162915

https://metro.co.uk/2020/10/30/employees-must-acknowledge-white-privilege-to-make-workplaces-better-for-minority-staff-13507313/

https://www.apa.org/news/podcasts/speaking-of-psychology/white-privilege

https://www.rezrunner.com/blog/how-to-handle-interview-rejections/

https://www.geeksforgeeks.org/interview-rejections-how-to-handle/

https://www.voicesofyouth.org/blog/staying-true-yourself

https://blog.sivanaspirit.com/mf-gn-important-reasons-why-you-should-be-true-to-yourself/

https://www.forbes.com/sites/amymorin/2014/11/23/7-scientifically-proven-benefits-of-gratitude-that-will-motivate-you-to-give-thanks-year-round/

Notes

Notes

Notes

Notes

Notes

Notes

Megan Wellman, a native of Bournemouth, is an author who draws on her extensive travels and diverse upbringing to infuse her writing with a distinct perspective. Her experiences as a mixed-race woman navigating professional challenges have fueled her passion for advocating inclusive workplaces.

Currently dividing her time between Bournemouth and London, Megan's work echoes the contrasts between coastal and urban life. Her writing delves into the complexities of identity, equality, and inclusiveness, inviting readers to reflect on these pertinent themes.

Through her words, she prompts readers to consider society's approach to diversity and its potential evolution.

Printed in Great Britain
by Amazon